THE EMBERS
THE BOBBY TOMLINSON STORY

*Passion, Perseverance, and
The Power of Music*

CHRIS JONES, BILL BENNERS, & SKIP CRAYTON

McBryde Publishing
NEW BERN, NORTH CAROLINA USA

McBryde Publishing
2419 Turtle Bay Drive
New Bern, North Carolina 28562
252-670-6709

Copyright © 2024 by Chris Jones, Bill Benners, & Skip Crayton

All rights reserved. No part of this book may be reprinted, reproduced, or utilized in any form or by any electronic, mechanical, or other means, now known or hereafter invented, including photocopying and recording, or in any information storage or retrieval system, without permission in writing from the publishers except in the case of brief quotations embodied in critical articles and reviews.

Printed in the United States of America
Published in 2024 by McBryde Publishing, a subsidiary of Benners Studio, Inc.

First Paperback Edition, 2024

Library of Congress Control Number: 2024919575

Paperback ISBN: 978-1-73398-245-0

www.mcbrydepublishing.com

TABLE OF CONTENTS

Dedication v
Chapter 1 – The Journey 3
Chapter 2 - Meet Bobby Tomlinson 6
Chapter 3 - Meeting Jackie Gore 11
Chapter 4 – Taking Raleigh by Storm 15
Chapter 5 – The Five Jays 20
Chapter 6 – Naming The Band 25
Chapter 7 – Early Gigs 30
Chapter 8 – Jim Thornton's Dance Club 34
Chapter 9 – Going Pro 40
Chapter 10 – WKIX "Men of Music" 44
Chapter 11 – Playing with the Big Boys 50
Chapter 12 – The First Embers Club 57
Chapter 13 – B Caudle 61
Chapter 14 – Atlantic Beach 68
Chapter 15 – The Embers Beach Club 73
Chapter 16 – New Opportunities 81
Chapter 17 – Floor Shows 89
Chapter 18 – The Landmark Resort 97
Chapter 19 – People Come, People Go 103
Chapter 20 – The Embers Hilton Underground 106
Chapter 21 – "I Love Beach Music" 111
Chapter 22 – Extended Play Medleys 118
Chapter 23 – Someone Handed Jackie a Beer 122
Chapter 24 – The Budweiser Years 126
Chapter 25 – Making Waves 132

Chapter 26 – The Embers' Golden Years.................. 138
Chapter 27 – Those Golden 80s 143
Chapter 28 – Touring the Southeast........................ 150
Chapter 29 - The Wave Crests.................................. 158
Chapter 30 – Egos and Dissention 165
Chapter 31 – Resilience and Reinvention................. 172
Chapter 32 – New Sounds.. 176
Chapter 33 – The Mid-90s.. 182
Chapter 34 – The Late 90s 187
Chapter 35 – Live at the Sands 194
Chapter 36 – The Bluewater Years 198
Chapter 37 – More Bluewater.................................. 205
Chapter 38 – Christmas Shows and Korea 210
Chapter 39 – Craig Woolard Returns...................... 216
Chapter 40 – T.J. Lubinsky....................................... 220
Chapter 41 – Bobby Steps Away.............................. 224
Chapter 42 – Northern Soul 228
Epilogue 235
Acknowledgments.. 241
About the Authors 245
To Chris Jones 249
Members of the Band... 251
Embers Crew & Specialist Members....................... 253
Embers' Bluewater Investors................................... 255
Embers' Sponsors... 257
Special Recognition.. 259
INDEX 261

DEDICATION

This book is lovingly dedicated to my family, whose unwavering support has been the foundation of my life and career.

To my dear parents, Josh and Ruth Tomlinson, known affectionately as "Mr. and Mrs. T," thank you for instilling in me the values of hard work, dedication, and perseverance. Your love and guidance have been my compass throughout this incredible journey.

To my brother, John Tomlinson, your friendship and encouragement have always meant the world to me. Thank you for standing by my side every step of the way.

With love and gratitude,

Bobby Tomlinson

Chapter 1

THE JOURNEY OF THE EMBERS, one of North Carolina's most beloved bands, is a story of passion, perseverance, and the power of music to bring people together. Since 1958, The Embers have been at the heart and soul of Carolina Beach Music, captivating audiences with their infectious rhythms and soulful melodies. Their music has become the soundtrack to countless memories, from sun-soaked days on the beach to lively nights on the dance floor.

At the center of this remarkable journey is Bobby Tomlinson, one of the band's founding members and their drummer for more than six decades. Bobby's love for music began at an early age, and it was his unwavering dedication, organizational skills, and talent that helped shape The Embers into the iconic band they are today. Through his and other members' eyes, we will explore the highs and lows, the triumphs and challenges, and the moments that have defined The Embers' legacy.

This chronicle is a tribute to The Embers and their enduring impact on the world of music. It delves into their history, from their humble beginnings in the late 1950s to their rise to fame, and the unique sound that has made them a staple of Carolina Beach Music. It is also a personal journey as Bobby Tomlinson shares his memories, insights, and reflections on a lifetime spent in music.

This work journeys through Bobby's childhood introduction to drumming, the early days of the band, where passion and determination fueled their dreams, to the first notes of what would become their signature sound beginning to take shape. We'll revisit their rise to fame with unforgettable performances and beloved regional hits that made them legends in the Carolina Beach Music scene. We'll explore the dynamics within the band, the changing lineup, and the unique contributions of its outstanding members.

Through Bobby's and other members', associates', and historians' own words, including those collected by Skip Crayton and Bill Benners during the making of their documentary film *The Embers – The Heart and Soul of Beach Music,* readers are granted an even more intimate backstage pass to life on the road, the excitement of touring, and the unbreakable bond formed with fans over the years. We'll dive into the creative process behind their recordings, providing an overview of their discography. This work will also shine a light on the community of fans who have supported them through the years, making them more than just a band, but a beloved institution.

The story of The Embers is not just about music, it's about the people who made it all possible, the friendships forged, the challenges overcome, and the legacy that continues to inspire new generations. As we explore their journey, you'll gain a deeper appreciation for the music that has brought joy to so many and the man who has been at the heart of it all.

Welcome to the world of The Embers, as seen through the eyes of those who lived it and loved it. Whether you're a long-time fan or new to their music, there's something here for everyone.

Chapter 2

THE STORY OF THE EMBERS begins with Bobby Tomlinson, and Bobby Tomlinson's story begins in Wilson, North Carolina, where he was born in his grandfather's house in October of 1940. But it wasn't long before his family moved to Goldsboro where his father worked at Dewey Brothers Foundry manufacturing manhole covers and heavy industrial items.

Despite battling severe asthma, a condition that caused him to miss a significant amount of school and led to him failing first grade, Bobby's resilience shone through. He vividly remembers the day he first encountered the captivating sound of a marching band. It was the drummers' snare drum "street beat" and the steady "boom, boom, boom" of the big bass drum that drew him in.

Living just two blocks from downtown, he ran to find them. He was six or seven years old—just a kid. There was a crowd lined up three or four deep on the street, but Bobby squeezed his way in. The band's blue and silver uniforms sparkled in the sun, making them stand out from the crowd.

The Goldsboro High School Marching Band, known as The Marching Earthquakes, had stopped in front of the Paramount Theatre to perform an impromptu concert. Bobby nosed through the crowd and came up beside the drum section. That was Bobby's first encounter with drums and he was hooked.

"I watched them and I couldn't believe it. Those drums just fascinated me. I vividly recall the allure of their rhythmic beats echoing through the streets. Music became my passion, my solace, and my purpose."

Growing up in Goldsboro significantly influenced Bobby's early musical journey. Around the age of ten, he heard an announcement on the PA system at William Street Elementary School. "If you are interested in playing in the band, report to the gymnasium tomorrow morning."

"So, I went home and told my mother I wanted to play in the band. She gave me fifty cents and sent me to get a rudiments book and a pair of drumsticks."

The next day, Bobby walked into the gymnasium, its polished wooden floors gleaming under the harsh fluorescent lights. The buzz of chatter filled the space, creating a symphony of anticipation. He joined the line that had formed, his heart pounding in his chest.

As he inched closer to the front, the imposing figure of John B. Thompson came into view. The band director's stern expression softened slightly as he addressed each hopeful student.

When it was Bobby's turn, Mr. Thompson's eyes met his with a curious glint. "Young man, what would you like to play?" he asked.

"Drums," Bobby said emphatically.

But the director's response was a blow. "Well, I only take fourteen and I already have fourteen."

Disappointment washed over Bobby, his eyes welling up with unbidden tears. "If I can't play drums, I don't want to play nothing!" he declared, his voice trembling with emotion.

Mr. Thompson's gaze softened, and he handed over a drumstick. "Tap on the desk," he instructed. The rhythmic tapping echoed in the silent gymnasium. After a moment, Mr. Thompson nodded, "You've got pretty good meter. I'm going to make you number fifteen."

Under John Thompson's tutelage, Bobby quickly picked up the drums and, although still in junior high school, it wasn't long before Thompson called Bobby up to march with the varsity band. Bobby and several other William Street schoolmates would ride their bicycles to the high school to join the senior high Marching Earthquakes Band, blurring the lines between junior and senior high school experiences.

This early exposure to advanced musical settings further fueled his lust for drumming and cemented his commitment to music.

"The most exciting day of my life was the day I strapped on a snare drum at age fourteen, two years younger than anybody in the Goldsboro High School Band, and marched down South Center Street. That's the day I fell in love with the drums."

Thompson's mentorship extended beyond musical instruction. He imparted invaluable life lessons and became a close friend. Bobby credits Thompson and his high school experiences with ingraining in him the importance of logistics, teamwork, and discipline—traits that accompanied him on his journey in professional music. Their bond endured even after he moved away.

Later, when Bobby co-founded The Embers, they would return to play in Goldsboro and Thompson would always come out to see him, fondly referring to him as "number fifteen."

In Goldsboro, one of Bobby's eighth-grade teachers introduced his class to a dance called "the bop," a hipper version of the swing dances from the 30s and 40s. They had lessons in the school gym, following a little book with diagrams showing how to move their feet and dance. Despite the common aversion to dancing among boys his age, Bobby enjoyed it.

Woodland Lake, later renamed Gold Park Lake, was a popular hangout spot on the outskirts of Dudley. It was a one-story wooden building with windows all around with shutters open to let the breeze flow through—much like one would see at the beach. It was there that the dancers would meet up and practice their moves.

There was always sand on the floor tracked in from outside. Every time you took a step or made a move, it sounded like sandpaper. "Music to my ears," said Tomlinson.

"The first song I heard on that jukebox when I walked in was 'Wine Spo-De-O-Dee.' All the music on the juke was what my buddies and I heard at night on John R's or Bill "Hossman" Allen's show on WLAC, a radio station based in Nashville, Tennessee."

At that time, mainstream radio was dominated by country music, but Bobby and his friends, like Roger Wise and Philip Littleton, were really into Black music. Gathering at Philip's house, they listened to 45 rpm records.

"They had all these great records," Bobby recalled. "Especially the Atco and Atlantic labels with songs by The Coasters and The Drifters. One of the songs that sticks out is a song called 'Ling Ting Tong' by The Five Keys."

Despite the racial segregation of radio at the time, they were drawn to the "rhythm and blues" music played on WLAC.

"We would listen to those songs and we'd order them. They'd have a James Brown special and they'd sell you three James Brown records with an 8x10 suitable for framing. But we were kids and we just stayed glued to that radio station."

Life took a significant turn when Bobby was fifteen. His family relocated to Raleigh where his father was offered a managerial position at the Foundry. Initially disappointed to leave his mentor, the move to Raleigh ultimately became the catalyst for his musical roots to grow deep.

CHAPTER 3

THE MOVE TO RALEIGH turned Bobby's world upside down. On one hand, he was glad his father got the new job at the Foundry. But for Bobby, big changes were ahead for him. He would not only have to adjust to a new school and make new friends this year, but because of the way the school system was set up, he would need to switch to yet another new school the following year.

In the fall of 1955, Bobby Tomlinson enrolled in the ninth grade at Hugh Morson Junior High School. But due to the configuration of Raleigh's middle schools and high schools, he was not be able to "play up" with the senior high band as he had done in Goldsboro.

Hugh Morson was a large, three-story building built in the 1920s in Gothic architectural style complete with gargoyles. It housed over twelve hundred students in grades seven through nine.

The band and music rooms were on the third floor—places Bobby would get to know well.

As luck would have it, there was another newcomer at Hugh Morson that year. Jackie Gore, a musically gifted seventh-grader, had also enrolled that fall. Although Bobby was eighteen months older, their paths were destined to cross soon. They shared a common love of contemporary music.

Bobby Tomlinson was a young man with a soul steeped in rhythm and a heart that beat in perfect time. He had been nurtured by a proud school band director in Goldsboro. His nimble fingers, trained through countless hours on the drums, could coax melodies from the simplest of beats, transforming ordinary moments into stirring experiences. Goldsboro had been his playground and now Raleigh beckoned with the promise of new adventures.

Jackie Gore, on the other hand, was a vocalist with perfect pitch whose voice could melt the coldest of hearts and elevate the spirits of anyone who had the privilege of listening. Raised on the soulful strains of gospel and the infectious grooves of rhythm and blues, Jackie had honed his craft in church but loved getting on the stage in front of his fellow students where every note was a testament to his unwavering passion for music.

"Hugh Morson was different from any other school I was familiar with," recalled Bobby. "They had a gymnasium near the lunchroom and students would congregate in the gym after lunch. 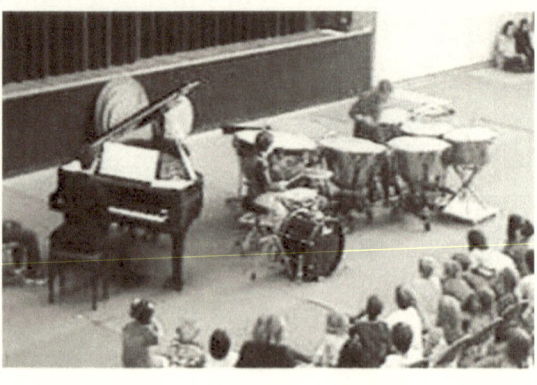 It had a jukebox full of rhythm and blues music. I mean, they had Little Richard on that jukebox. It also had an auditorium with a set of drums backstage and a piano.

"The first day of school I went to the gymnasium and I'm standing back watching everybody. The music's playing, but nobody's dancing. And these two girls started talking to me.

"One of them asked, 'you dance?' I said, 'Yeah, I dance a little bit.' I got out there and, all of a sudden, I had everybody circling around me watching." Bobby's fashion was different. "I wore pink pants with peg legs—straight out of American Graffiti. And right off, everybody's talking about this strange-looking guy who can dance. So, every day at lunchtime, I was like the center of attraction for a long time."

At the same time, Jackie Gore was making a name for himself in seventh grade. "I've been singing since I was a little kid in Sunday school," Jackie said. "Back when I was five and six years old, that's when I started singing. And my mother and daddy were very good singers and I guess that's where I got my talent.

"And when I was in the fourth grade in Durham, I started playing cornet, which is a smaller version of a trumpet. When I was in the sixth grade, I entered a talent contest which I won singing a song called 'The Dark Town Strutters Ball' and playing my cornet. And to have all of those kids standing at the end of the stage screaming for me when I won the talent show, I knew at twelve years old what I was going to be doing for the rest of my life."

At Morson, Jackie, Bobby, and a few others began jamming daily in the gymnasium at lunchtime. Bobby recalled. "We put together a little band. We had a washtub bass instead of a regular bass. We weren't very good, but we had a good time."

Chapter 4

By the time Bobby was ready for tenth grade, he transitioned to Needham Broughton High School. Situated in the northwestern part of town, this tenth through twelfth grade institution housed two thousand students, creating a bustling environment ripe with opportunities for young musicians.

Bobby Tomlinson was thrilled to finally be able to try out for the senior high school band. However, this move involved the merging graduates of two distinct junior high schools—Hugh Morson and Josephus Daniels—into the high school sophomore year. And the new band director had called for full-scale tryouts to sort things out.

Undeterred by the challenge, Bobby approached the tryouts with determination and confidence, drawing on his strong musical background from the William Street and Goldsboro High School bands. The competitive atmosphere was palpable as students showcased their skills, each hoping to impress the new director and secure their place in the band. Despite the stiff competition, Bobby's talent and hard work paid off. His exceptional drumming skills shone through, earning him the prestigious "first chair" in 1957.

Bobby was in the Broughton High School "Marching 100," as it was called, the symphonic band, and a smaller band called the "Circus Band" that played at sporting events.

He would be named Band Captain in his 1958-59 senior year. He would be referred to in his senior yearbook as "Red man, drummer, and dancing champ." These achievements were not only a testament to his dedication but also a significant milestone in his musical journey, marking him as a standout talent even among his peers.

Bobby's burgeoning reputation as a "hotshot drummer" reverberated through the local music scene. Word of his talent spread like flame on gasoline, reaching the ears of musicians and enthusiasts alike. This recognition led to a pivotal moment in Bobby's young career—his first professional drumming experience.

The opportunity came unexpectedly with a call that would change the trajectory of his musical journey. A local band, intrigued by the buzz surrounding this young prodigy, invited Bobby to join them for a performance. At just sixteen years old, Bobby was thrilled at the prospect of playing with seasoned musicians, seeing it as a chance to hone his skills and gain invaluable experience.

Equipped with his own drum set, Bobby eagerly joined the group of country musicians. He didn't anticipate that this experience would be more than just another chance to play. It was to be his first paid gig. As he was whisked away to the venue, a mix of excitement and nerves coursed through him. The night was filled with the lively twang of country melodies and Bobby's drumming added a vibrant rhythm that elevated the performance.

The culmination of the evening came not just from the applause of the audience, but from a tangible reward. As the night drew to a close and Bobby began to pack up his drum set, the band members approached him with a humble, yet, significant token of appreciation—a five-dollar bill.

It was a moment of both surprise and pride for Bobby. He had expected nothing more than the joy of playing, but this unexpected payment marked his transition from an amateur enthusiast to a professional musician.

Filled with a sense of accomplishment, Bobby excitedly shared the news with his father. Holding up the crisp five-dollar bill, he recounted the evening's events with a glow of pride. The money, though modest, symbolized a milestone in his musical journey, a recognition of his talent, and the beginning of a new chapter in his career.

His father, sharing in his excitement, acknowledged this significant step with heartfelt congratulations. This moment not only bolstered Bobby's confidence but also fueled his determination to pursue his passion for drumming with even greater fervor.

Tomlinson soon found himself amid a significant business milestone, both for his career and for the history of a well-known American brand. He had been invited to play drums backing up a country music legend for the grand opening of the first Lowe's hardware store in North Wilkesboro, North Carolina.

The event was set to be a grand affair, and to add to its allure, Bobby would drum for country music royalty—Homer Briarhopper and Clyde Moody.

"When I first started listening to music in the early to mid-50s, Homer Briarhopper was all over the radio," Bobby reflected. "And Clyde Moody, who played guitar and bass, was also a good singer. He had played at the Grand Ole Opry with Bill Monroe and was a member of The Blue Grass Boys for several years. Moody played on Bill Monroe's 'Tennessee Waltz' back in the 1950s, which sold over two million records."

As Bobby recalled, the scene at Lowe's was nothing short of spectacular. The store, which had started as Lowe's North Wilkesboro Hardware in the 1920s, was now unveiling its first official branch, which has now become one of the largest building supply chains in America. The event was bustling with excitement. Homer Briarhopper and Clyde Moody—dressed in their vibrant Porter Wagoner suits and large cowboy hats—were the stars of the show. Their presence was a nod to the rich heritage of country music and its deep roots in the American South.

These men were more than musicians, they were icons whose careers spanned decades and whose music had defined an era. Briarhopper's charm and Moody's guitar picking created an electric atmosphere, drawing crowds from all over to witness this unique blend of commerce and culture.

For Bobby, playing alongside these legends was a surreal experience. He described the scene vividly, recalling how the crowd cheered and the music flowed seamlessly. The grand opening was more than just a commercial event, it was a celebration of community, music, and the entrepreneurial spirit that Lowe's represented.

This experience, rich with the sounds of guitars, steel strings, and rhythmic drumming, was a defining moment in Bobby's burgeoning career, one that he would remember fondly for years to come.

CHAPTER 5

BY 1957, ROCK 'N' ROLL, that new sound that burst on the scene in the mid-1950s, was in full swing. Artists like Elvis Presley, Little Richard, Chuck Berry, and Buddy Holly were at the forefront of this musical revolution. Rebellious lyrics and energetic performances regularly made the news and captivated the youth, challenging the conservative norms of the time.

Rhythm and blues (R&B) emerged as a major force on the Southern music scene. Artists like Ray Charles, Fats Domino, and Sam Cooke were crucial in shaping this genre.

Country music and bluegrass continued to thrive with artists like Hank Williams, Bill Monroe, and Johnny Cash achieving widespread acclaim. New sounds were coming out of Memphis and New Orleans—the blues. Artists like B.B. King and Muddy Waters emerged. And, of course, the South loved jazz. Louis Armstrong, Count Basie, and Duke Ellington toured religiously.

It was an era in which, despite the segregation policies, there was a degree of cultural integration underway. Music was a unifying force that brought together people from different backgrounds and broke down racial barriers. Integrated performances and radio shows were emerging.

In the summer of 1957, Bobby Tomlinson and Jackie Gore joined a band—Gene Fowler and The Falcons. Gene, a charismatic singer, led the group with a natural flair. Richard Dupree played the guitar and Mel Strickland played a steel guitar. Jackie joined with guitar in hand while Bobby provided the rhythmic backbone on drums. The Falcons primarily played country music, performing at local venues like the VFW, where smoky air and clinking glasses created a lively atmosphere.

"Mel told me one night that we had the only rock and roll steel guitar in the Carolinas," Tomlinson recalled. "I thought that was hilarious."

Recalling one of their early performances, Bobby chuckled, "We had to play one night and Gene picked us up," Bobby reminisced. "We went on stage and Gene came out wearing a white sport coat with a pink carnation. He sang Marty Robbins' 'A White Sport Coat (and a Pink Carnation)' song probably three or four times that night." The image of Gene in his striking outfit, passionately belting out the lyrics, remained etched in Bobby's memory.

Yet, Bobby and Jackie yearned for more. Their musical tastes were evolving, influenced by the electric sounds of the era.

In the fall of 1957, as Bobby entered his junior year, he and Jackie formed their own band.

Jackie's older brother, Randy Gore, was recruited on washtub bass, Jimmy Florence played the trumpet, and Jack Sullivan added his piano skills. They christened themselves "The Satellites," a very timely name at the start of the Space Age.

Their early performances were a blend of youthful exuberance and raw talent. They played at school dances, local gatherings, and any event that would have them. Their repertoire included covers of popular hits and instrumentals of the day, all delivered with a contagious enthusiasm.

One memorable day at Jack Sullivan's house, they stumbled upon a piece of family stationery titled "5 J's," listing the names of the five family members, all of whom had a "J" in their name. Inspired by this coincidence, they rebranded themselves as "The Five Jays." The new name soon featured a new lineup. Randy Gore, Jimmy Florence, and Jack Sullivan left the band, making way for Ken Barnes on bass, Gene Jones on saxophone, and Blair Ellis on piano.

Ken Barnes brought an actual bass fiddle to the band. It was one of those tall, floor-standing models. Gene Jones was a very talented individual who would soon be heading to the Cincinnati Conservatory of Music. He composed an instrumental song the band included in its set lists in early 1958.

Blair was a year older than the others and had come from a local quartet named The Escorts, bringing with him a Wurlitzer piano, a wealth of experience, and a refined touch on the keys. Blair stood up when he played. The Five Jays, as they were now known, would soon make a name for themselves in the local music scene.

They became a fixture at local sock hops, debutante parties, and high school proms. One of Bobby's favorite memories was The Five Jays playing an event at Village Theatre. "It was a Pepsi-Cola-sponsored concert," Tomlinson said. "Admission was ten Pepsi bottle caps."

The Five Jays performed everywhere they could, their youthful faces and infectious music leaving an indelible mark on the local scene. Amidst their hectic schedule, they even found time to record two records, a significant achievement for a group of high school students.

Around this time, The Five Jays were approached by a local songwriter and a friend from an earlier band with a proposition. George Bailey, along with Mel Strickland—the steel guitar player they had played with while in Gene Fowler and the Falcons—had penned several original songs and wanted four of them to be recorded by a vocal quartet, The Juniors, comprised of Donald King, Bill Duncan, Ken Pierce, and Simon Dixon. But Bailey wanted them backed with a band. Donald's quartet provided the vocals and The Five Jays provided the musical accompaniment.

They all gathered at the WRAL radio studios in downtown Raleigh—a place steeped in history and the scent of old vinyl records. There, they recorded four songs under the Rose-Beth label, named after the songwriter's two daughters. The labels on the two 45s, "I Love My Baby/A Touch of Gentleness" and "Money, Money, Money/Once In a Blue Moon, credited singer Donald King with The Four Juniors and The Five Jays.

"We were just a bunch of high school students, but we had already produced two records," Bobby said, a proud glimmer in his eyes. "It felt like a significant accomplishment back then. Yeah, that was a big deal."

Although those recordings did not catapult them to instant stardom, they got them attention. They were on a pair of records. Recording in a professional studio was invaluable, providing them with a glimpse into the world of professional music. It was a stepping stone, a promise of greater things to come.

Chapter 6

THE EARLY YEARS were a total whirlwind as the band was still part-time and the members had regular day jobs, but they still managed to keep the band alive. Jackie worked as a painter and as a shoe salesman. Bobby worked at a wholesale pharmaceutical business and office supply company.

As they navigated their high school years, playing for high school and college events remained their main course. They played with heart and soul, their music resonating with audiences everywhere they played. And for Bobby, Jackie, and The Five Jays, the journey was nearing an end.

As the 1957-58 school year came to a close, Ken Barnes was leaving for the Air Force and Gene Jones was headed to the Cincinnati Conservatory of Music. Bobby would be a senior in high school that fall. Blair continued his studies at NC State and Jackie had married his high school sweetheart, LaRue Byrd.

The departure of Ken and Gene left only Jackie, Blair, and Bobby in the band. With the band in transition, it seemed a good time to explore a name change.

Bobby, Jackie, and Blair gathered at Blair's house on Harvey Street. Bobby suggested the need for a new name that would stand out and be appropriate for venues like country clubs, ritzy nightclubs, and grand concert halls.

Bobby remembers carrying a stack of 45s that day. Among them was The Five Satins' "In the Still of the Night" on Ember Records. The logo on the record— flaming logs spelling out the name "Ember  Records"—ignited an idea. "Why don't we call ourselves 'The Embers?" Bobby suggested, his voice brimming with excitement.

Blair Ellis remembered the naming event differently. "I named them," he told McBryde Films in 2010 during a filmed interview for the upcoming documentary film on The Embers. Ellis explained, "What happened was— between Chapel Hill and Greensboro, there's a restaurant called 'The Embers.' And I kept looking at that restaurant, 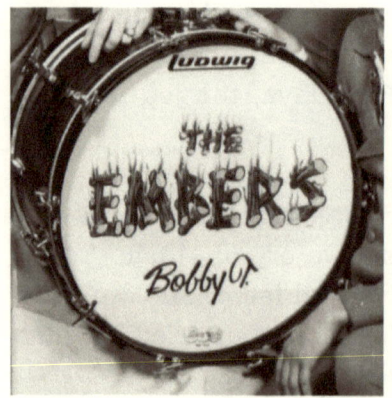 The Embers, and I said, that might be a good name for the band."

Regardless of the origin, the name struck a chord, resonating with the band's collective vision. "The Embers" it was. And, they adopted a logo with flaming logs to spell out their name, painting it boldly on the bass drum and the equipment trailer, a symbol of their burning ambition. And then, there was the matter of needing an additional musician.

Back when they were still The Five Jays, Bobby had occasionally hired a Black saxophone player, Doug Harrison, to fill in when Ken and Gene were out touring colleges. Doug, who was almost thirty years old while the others were barely eighteen, blew them away with his playing. Tomlinson said, "When I auditioned Doug, he opened his saxophone case in the corner and started warming up and I'd never heard anything like that. So, I recommended hiring Doug, even though it was a racially charged time."

The band decided it didn't matter and hired Doug, forming an integrated quartet with Blair on piano and bass piano, Doug on saxophone, Jackie on guitar and vocals, and Tomlinson on drums.

The Embers had a unique sound they stumbled upon when Jackie purchased a Les Paul guitar with a stereophonic guitar amplifier. During practice one day, Blair plugged his Wurlitzer electric piano into Jackie's stereophonic amplifier and the sound burst into a new dimension. Add that to Doug's great saxophone work and The Embers were on their way.

Their first gig with Doug was a fraternity house party for Blair's Kappa Sigma fraternity at NC State. This opened a crucial gateway for the band. Blair's fraternity connections not only kept them busy with local high school and college events but also helped The Embers break into the wider fraternity circuit, where they found themselves frequently performing at Kappa Sig houses on campuses across the region. This exposure proved to be an essential passage for many young bands like The Embers, giving them access to larger, enthusiastic audiences.

Their performances were electric, filled with the energy and excitement of a band finding its groove. They played songs by James Brown, Little Richard, Bobby Bland, and Louis Armstrong, as well as "You Can't Sit Down," a great upbeat dance number by The Phil Upchurch Combo from the 1950s. The audiences loved them and their popularity soared.

Doug Harrison was an amazing musician, but sometimes racial issues came up. Event organizers complained about their Black sax player. This added a layer of tension and uncertainty to their performance.

They were hired for a party in New Bern, and the person booking the event made it clear they wanted an all-white band and expressed concern about their Black saxophone player. Tomlinson explained Doug was from Puerto Rico and then told Doug to say "No Speak English" if anyone tried to talk to him.

The party was drama-free and Doug nailed his performance, including backup vocals in English on several songs.

No one said a word.

Chapter 7

THE EMBERS, a versatile quartet, distinguished themselves in an era where larger ensembles dominated the stage. Their unique formation, a mere four-piece band amidst a sea of five-piece groups and beyond, forged a harmonious blend that resonated with an almost magical clarity. Each member contributed a distinct voice to their collective melody, and their musical skills by this time were to a point where they could cover just about any song you heard on the radio.

Blair spoke about the trouble they had harmonizing in the beginning. "When we were trying to harmonize, I would pick a note and Bobby would sing the same note. Then, if I harmonized with that note, as soon as I got on the harmonic note, Bobby would move up to the harmonic note. Then I would have to back down to the first note and then he'd move back down there. So, we could not harmonize."

Eventually, harmonizing became one of the finest traits of The Embers.

"And we sounded pretty darn good," said Tomlinson. "After we started playing at Blair's fraternity house, Kappa Sig at NC State, word got around to other fraternities on campus and, of course, some UNC fraternity brothers would also be around. Soon, we started drawing a crowd. And we started charging the fraternities and that started us on our way."

"It didn't take long before we got overwhelmed playing three or four nights a week," said Tomlinson. "There weren't but two or three bands around. Us, Doug Clark and The Hot Nuts, and one or two more. And we did well and started getting more and more jobs."

The college party scene was demanding, keeping the band constantly on the road. It could be grueling, with some events spanning entire weekends and involving multiple performances. On one occasion, they played seven times over three days.

The college circuit provided numerous opportunities for weekend gigs, including fraternity parties, Big Sister Dances, Pledge Weekends, Senior Days, Founder's Weekends, Spring Formals, Mardi Gras Parties at Peace College, football and basketball weekend events, and homecomings. Interspersed with these were local events such as country club parties, cotillions, and debutante balls. The band played them all.

As The Embers were trailblazers in race relations for that time, having an integrated band in the Jim Crow era brought a few headaches. The Embers had to navigate the challenges of finding suitable accommodations for their Black sax player during their travels, highlighting the racial divide of the time and the difficulties they faced.

"It was a weird time," said Tomlinson. "If we were playing out of town, say a fraternity party, and it was too far to get home or there was another event the next day that was nearby, we would get a hotel room. There weren't Black hotels in most places at that time. We would arrange for Doug to stay with the fraternity house helpers. He would spend the night and we would pick him up the next day."

Often traveling at night, the band would drive back to Raleigh from out-of-town gigs, tuning in to WLAC, the station they listened to growing up. They listened to the records on the radio, ordered them, and learned the songs introducing music that was usually unknown locally. One notable song was "Candy" by the Astors, which audiences often assumed was their original piece.

In the fall of 1961, The Embers were in a studio working on what would become their first release under their new name. They met Marshall Sehorn through their friend Buddy Skipper, who had met Sehorn when Skipper's band, The Jetty Jumpers, frequently played on the Carolina coast in the late 1950s. Buddy had recorded a 45 for Marshall's label.

Marshall heard The Embers one night and decided to record them for his label, Ace Records, out of Jackson, Mississippi. Interestingly, their first song was a Christmas tune. At the time, there was a popular dance called "The Shimmy," and the band incorporated this phrase into the standard "Winter Wonderland."

They recorded the song at Green's Studio in Durham, the only available time being around two or three o'clock in the morning.

The band went in the middle of the night, following Doug Clark and The Hot Nuts, who had just wrapped up what was likely the recording session for their first LP for Gross Records, "Nuts To You," which would feature their soon-to-be signature song, "Hot Nuts, Get 'Em From The Peanut Man."

The Embers recorded their song at around three in the morning. The resulting single was (Shimmying in a) "Winter Wonderland," backed with "I'm So Lonely," released under the name "The Swinging Embers featuring Jackie Hamilton," which was Jackie Gore's middle name. The songs were officially released in January 1962 as Ace Records #644 although the songs were getting airplay before the end of 1961. This marked their first national release, and Ace was a prominent label at the time which further helped promote the band.

Jim Thornton, a well-known local celebrity with his own television show on WTVD called "Jim Thornton's Saturday Night Country Style," had only hosted country music acts at his club, Jim Thornton's Dance Club. Tomlinson approached Thornton suggesting that The Embers had a sound he might like despite his usual preference for country music.

When asked about their style, Tomlinson explained that The Embers played a mix of popular and Black music. Although skeptical, Thornton offered a deal—The Embers could take the door earnings while he would keep the bar revenue. Tomlinson agreed, and the deal was on.

Chapter 8

The Embers' first appearance at Jim Thornton's Dance Club drew about seventy-five people at seventy-five cents per entry, with Bobby's father managing the door. To simplify transactions, they charged a dollar the following week. Within four to five weeks, the crowd had grown to three hundred people per night, establishing The Embers as a major attraction at Jim Thornton's Dance Club.

"That really put us on the map because people came from all over to hear us play," Tomlinson said. "And it wasn't beach music. Back then, it was known as rhythm and blues and Black music." He continued, "While he had us there, he started bringing in national acts on Wednesday nights. We were already playing Black music and we were doing a good job. But then we actually played with nationally known Black musicians."

The band would arrive at the club around five o'clock to rehearse for a couple of hours with the guest artists. The format was straightforward—The Embers would open the evening with a set, and then bring out the guest artists for their set. This cycle would repeat, providing a dynamic and varied performance. Practicing and performing with national artists was an invaluable experience for the band.

One of the first groups they shared the stage with was The Marcels, best known for their hit "Blue Moon." Despite their fame, The Marcels had primarily performed on touring shows like Dick Clark's Caravan of Stars, where bands typically played only one or two songs.

Consequently, the Marcels had a limited repertoire. Realizing this, The Embers encouraged The Marcels to expand their set list, helping them learn several new songs.

The Embers also had the opportunity to play with notable artists like Clarence "Frogman" Henry, Jerry Lee Lewis, and Fats Domino. These artists were quite popular at the time and performing with them allowed the band to refine their skills and improve their craft. This period of collaboration and performance was crucial in honing their abilities and solidifying their reputation.

"One night," Blair Ellis explained, "we were backing The Clovers at Jim Thornton's and were rehearsing down in the basement. You can't believe how good a group like that sounds," said Ellis. "With no microphones, we played a song called 'Love Potion Number Nine.' And, it's a hard song to play and The Clovers said they could not perform that song often when being backed up by local bands like us because not many bands could do the song." But The Embers could. "That was one of the most exciting things," Ellis said. "To hear them sing that song live."

The Embers continued to perform regularly at Jim Thornton's Dance Club, becoming so popular that Thornton often booked them for entire weekends, drawing packed crowds.

It's a little-known story, but there was a female vocalist who sang with "The Swinging Embers" for several months during 1962. Her name was Janice Sinquefield, but her stage name was "Peaches." She was particularly popular at the time with the crowds at Jim Thornton's dance club.

Janice, who lived in Wilson, NC, contacted Bobby in 1961, wanting to sing with the band. Female singers in bands were uncommon at the time. Sharon (Henshaw) Copeland and Linda "Quig" Quinlan sang with The Monzas and Linda Griffith sang with The Castaways Combo. But, by and large, there were not that many female singers back then.

"She was a good singer and attractive," Tomlinson recalls. "She sounded a lot like Teresa Brewer who was very popular nationally at the time. That was her thing.

Tomlinson recalls The Embers covering Lavern Baker's "Tweedle Dee" with "Peaches" up front. "She did a good job and it went over well."

After a few months, The Embers decided to stay with the all-male lineup. Janice went on to sing and headline in Phoenix, Arizona for a while.

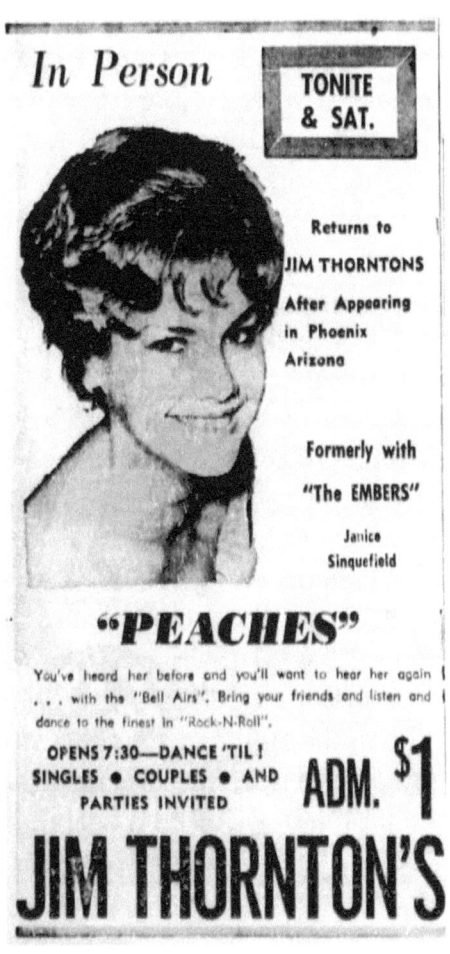

Jim Thornton liked her performances and brought her back in May for a few weeks with The Bell Airs. The May 18th advertisement cited her as "formerly with The Embers."

By the dawn of the 1960s, The Embers had become a force to be reckoned with, performing regularly at Jim Thornton's Dance Club in Raleigh and backing prominent national acts. Their evolving sound was gaining more attention.

With each passing year, The Embers continued to refine their act but, as is common in the music industry, personnel changes occurred. Doug Harrison left the band in 1961 due to the negative impact the busy Embers' schedule had on his marriage.

Doug was replaced on saxophone by Foy Biggers from Buddy Skipper and the Jetty Jumpers. Foy performed on the first Embers' LP "The Embers Roll Eleven" and remained with the band for two years.

After graduating from NC State in 1962, Blair Ellis left the band to pursue a career in chemical engineering, but not before helping to find his replacement. Blair placed an ad in the NC State student newspaper, and Dave Norket, a classically-trained pianist responded. "He really wanted that job," Blair said. "He practiced countless hours and learned to play the Ray Charles rendition of 'What'd I Say' well enough for an audition. And he got the job."

However, Norket was the fun-loving type and would partake of the spirits more than he should have. And soon, his partying got in the way of his Embers' schedule.

Durwood Martin recalls one of Dave Norket's wild times. "I was down at Atlantic Beach and The Embers were playing at the Pavilion back when the Masons had it. It was a Saturday night and I had said 'Hey' to Bobby and Jackie when I came in. And Dave Norket was playing the piano. Frank Reich was playing the saxophone.

The band, now renowned for their electrifying performances, often played at the Pavilion—a summer hotspot that magnetized crowds from all corners of eastern North Carolina. Bobby Tomlinson fondly recalls, "Every weekend we played, we packed the house. You couldn't get in the place. We played Friday nights,

Saturday nights, and Sunday afternoon. We were very popular in eastern North Carolina."

On one of those Saturday nights, Durwood recalled, "About the second set, I heard a voice on the PA system say, 'Hey, Durwood Martin, if you're still here, will you come up to the stage?'

"I went to the stage and found Norket had passed out and couldn't play. So, they asked if I could sit in. I said 'Yeah' because we all knew the same songs. I finished the night with The Embers and the next day, they had a job in the small town of Atlantic, just down the road, for an outdoor debutante party. I played for that, too, and thought it was pretty cool because I went to the beach with no money and ended up making some money while I was down there.

"Later that summer, I was doing construction work helping my dad and I was underneath an apartment complex that they were building putting insulation up in the rafters in about a two-inch space and I heard somebody down there at the little crawl space hole say 'Durwood, are you in there?' And it was Bobby and Jackie. And they said 'Hey, we want you to play.' And I said 'Great. I don't have any equipment.' They bought me a piano and a piano bass and I started playing with them.

"In the first two weeks that I played with them, all the jobs were east of Raleigh, down in New Bern, Jacksonville, and at the beach. And I lived at home in Princeton. I'd stand up by the road and they'd pick me up at the Esso Station there in Princeton. We'd head east and they'd drop me back off on their way back to Raleigh."

Chapter 9

As 1964 progressed, The Embers found themselves increasingly in demand. They regularly worked three nights a week, sometimes four, often starting on Wednesday nights and extending through the frat party weekends. Despite their burgeoning music career, the band members still held day jobs to make ends meet.

Bobby Tomlinson was still juggling his full-time job at W.H. King Drug Company. "We started out just playing Wednesday nights and frat parties," he recalls.

Jackie was still balancing his time between being a husband, a painter, and playing in a band. Other members had their jobs as well. Life was a hectic blend of music and work.

Then suddenly, the demand for The Embers surged. "We're working three, four, and five nights a week," Bobby remembered, the pace taking a toll on his health. "I'm working full-time and playing too, and I catch every cold that goes around. I wasn't real sick, just run down." The relentless schedule left him exhausted and frequently under the weather.

Concerned, Bobby visited his doctor who told him, "Bob, we can stop all this." The doctor explained that Bobby needed to make a crucial decision—either continue playing music or keep his job at King Drug Company. "If you stop one of those and get proper rest, you won't be sick all the time," the doctor advised. It was a clear, straightforward choice for Bobby, one that offered an easy out from his overextended lifestyle.

The doctor's ultimatum prompted Bobby to give his notice at work. Reflecting on his journey, Bobby believes it was all part of a larger plan. "From the very beginning when I moved to Goldsboro and met John Thompson, everything has been aiming toward one point—to keep advancing everything and making something good out of every bad," he mused. The Embers' story, in his view, is one of perseverance and progress turning challenges into opportunities.

The decision marked a turning point for The Embers. They transitioned from being part-time musicians with day jobs to full-time professional musicians, fully committing to their craft. "The story of The Embers is not just about me, but everybody that ever played in this band. Everybody," Bobby emphasized. "We've all been going toward one point, and we're still going toward that point."

With their newfound focus and determination, The Embers were ready to make it or break it with their music. The transition was not just a professional shift but a testament to their dedication and belief in their potential as musicians. The Embers embraced their roles as full-time artists, prepared to navigate the highs and lows of the music industry.

Reflecting on those early years, Durwood recalls certain events with a sense of nostalgia. "Bobby always had a new Grand Prix or a new Bonneville every year in those early days and we pulled a little old trailer that was just custom-made for the equipment. So, one weekend Bobby's car was broken down and Jackie borrowed his father-in-law's Chrysler. It was a big old four-door green Chrysler, and we hooked the trailer up to it. And we were playing in Columbia, South Carolina.

"The highway was different then. You couldn't go interstate. So, we're cruising along and everything's fine and we're coming into this little town—the first stoplight we got to—and Jackie hit the brakes and there were no brakes. I mean *no* brakes. It went to the floor and he was pulling the gear shift down trying to make it stop. And we didn't have anywhere to go. The stoplight was red. Cars were lined up and we had no brakes. We threw all four doors open and were all dragging our shoes on the pavement trying to stop it. And Jackie cut into a service station. I don't know how, but we finally got it stopped.

"I really have no idea what happened at that point. I don't know how we got the brakes fixed but I know we were dragging shoe leather all the way into that service station. I don't know if it helped or not but we got her slowed down.

"Another time," Durwood continued. "And this involves Jackie, and when you really get into funny stories, a lot are going to involve Jackie because he did some crazy stuff. We were playing in Charlotte at a hotel we played on a regular basis and we were doing the Motown Revue at that time and Jackie was doing his Marvin Gaye medley and the dance the "bump" was big at that time.

"There was a dance floor and a railing beyond it and then seats all the way back to the back of this place. So, Jackie goes out there and grabs a woman off the dance floor and drags her to the stage and it's just the spotlight on Jackie and her. And he was singing to her and he was doing the bump with her, and when the song ended, Jackie said, 'Let's have a big round of applause for my dance partner' and everybody clapped and he let her go and she walked away. And now he's singing a little more and we look over and the poor woman has bumped into the railing and then turned and bumped into the wall.

"Turns out the woman was sight impaired. Finally, her husband grabs her, takes her back around the railing, and sits her down. That was one of many, many funny things that happened with Jackie and the band."

Blair Ellis spilled the beans on another bit of crazy fun they got into. "We'd do crazy, stupid stuff like the time we got a pistol with some blanks in it. And after playing one night, we hopped out at a service station to get a drink on the way home. And in the parking lot, we acted like we got into a fight. And somebody pulled out that pistol and 'Bam! Bam!' Then Jackie fell down and we grabbed him and dragged him into the car and drove off. I don't know what those people thought. But, thank goodness, the cops didn't come after us."

CHAPTER 10

THE EARLY 1960s brought a whirlwind of change to the Carolina music scene, shaking up the local radio landscape in ways that would leave a lasting impact. During the day, listeners were accustomed to a familiar mix of country, gospel, and popular tunes. As schools let out and the afternoon sun dipped, the airwaves would dance with more vibrant popular songs, sprinkling in some soulful rhythm and blues.

But the real magic happened as night fell, when powerful stations from faraway cities like Nashville, Chicago, Fort Wayne, New Orleans, and New York City pierced through the static, introducing local ears to an exciting and diverse array of musical styles and unforgettable DJs. In addition to John R. on Nashville's WLAC, there was Cousin Brucie on WABC New York, Big Jack Armstrong, "The Fastest Tongue in the East" on WKYC in Cleveland, Barnie Pip on WCFL Chicago, and the legendary Wolfman Jack broadcasting on XERF, a Mexican radio station across the border from Del Rio, Texas, whose high-powered 150,000-watt border-blaster signal could be heard on the AM dial across most of the US at night.

This nightly invasion of new sounds ignited a spark, forever altering the region's musical DNA. Amidst this sonic revolution, Raleigh's own WKIX emerged as a beacon for the young and curious. Realizing that the Raleigh-Durham area was teeming with colleges and college students hungry for fresh and exciting music, WKIX took a bold step. They began spinning the hottest Top-40 hits, transforming the station into a must-listen-to for the youth. WKIX became the soundtrack of their lives introducing them to new music that transcended local boundaries.

The power of local radio stations like WKIX, combined with the groundbreaking sound of early rock 'n' rollers, paved the way for what would become a seismic shift in the music world—the British Invasion. By 1964, The Beatles, The Rolling Stones, and a wave of British acts swept the American charts, captivating listeners who had already been primed for new sounds.

For local bands like The Embers, the sudden demand for British hits was undeniable. Fans clamored for covers of songs from across the Atlantic and The Embers quickly adapted blending the raw energy of R&B with the fresh sounds of the British Invasion. This period of change didn't just influence their music, it shaped their identity with the band even sporting mop-head hairdos and off-beat British-inspired outfits.

Four lads from Liverpool created waves that crashed onto the American music landscape. And behind them were other British acts that wanted to tap the American buying power. The Beatles rocketed up the U.S. charts and became the most popular musical act of the time.

They never played a college concert in the U.S., but they did find adoring fans who wanted their records.

Other English musicians coming to America at that time included The Rolling Stones, The Dave Clark Five, Freddie and the Dreamers, Manfred Mann, The Hollies, The Animals, The Yardbirds, The Kinks, The Moody Blues, The Spencer Davis Group, Herman's Hermits, and more. These acts toured the U.S. during the 60s, including the American South. It was only a matter of time before these acts joined the American acts in the Carolinas.

Carolina bands, including The Embers, felt the impact almost overnight. Their appearances brought constant requests for Beatles or British band tunes, pushing local musicians to adapt. The Embers, ever versatile, quickly added covers of Beatles' hits, even including "All My Lovin'" on their first album. But they didn't stop at the music—the band fully embraced the British Invasion style.

"We'd get in character," Bobby Tomlinson recalled, "complete with mop-head black hair." Their look evolved just as much as their sound, with longer hair and a wardrobe that echoed the edgy, youthful style coming out of England. For a time, The Embers became a band that could switch between their beach music roots and the electric energy of the British Invasion, showing their ability to adapt to the musical waves of the moment.

This period of transformation laid the groundwork for their continued success, as they navigated the ever-changing music scene while staying true to their identity. It was during this period that The Embers became friends with the air personalities at WKIX. "We got to know some of the DJs—Charlie Brown, Bob Jones, Steve Roddy,

Michael Reineri, Larry Gardner, Rick Dees, Bob Kelly—they were all phenomenal and were hot as a pistol," Tomlinson recalled. "And they started playing our music."

Charlie Brown, the station's astute music director, began organizing sock hops booking bands to play for dances while the "KIX Men of Music" hosted the events. "We 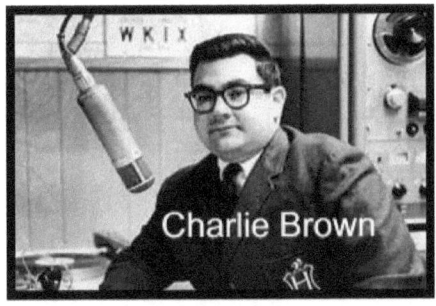 played for those," Bobby recalls. "It was all a trade-out. But we were on the radio. They weren't playing any other groups around here, so we were already successful. But this took us to another level. We owe a lot to WKIX, Charlie Brown, and the 'KIX Men of Music.'"

Music was changing. The Beatles had emerged, and The Embers' setlist had expanded beyond rhythm and blues. With the surge of LPs and more young people acquiring record players, the demand for an album grew. "Everyone kept saying, why don't you record an album?"

In May of 1964, The Embers collaborated with Jimmy Capps, one of the DJs at WKIX. "We were doing a show at NC State and Jimmy Capps set up his recording equipment and recorded what became our 'Embers  Roll Eleven' live album. He did the editing in his studio. Michael Reineri, one of the WKIX 'Men of Music,' introduced us and wrote the liner notes on the back of the album."

The album, released in the summer of 1964, encapsulated a typical Embers set, covering mostly R&B standards like Marvin Gaye's "Stubborn Kind of Fellow," The Impressions' "Gypsy Woman," The Coasters' "Searchin'," and The Embers' interpretation of the British Invasion, a cover of The Beatles, "All My Lovin."

Recording "The Embers Roll Eleven" marked a significant milestone for the band. "That live album captured the energy and excitement of our performances," Bobby explains. "It was a raw and authentic representation of our sound. Recording it live in the Ballroom of Erdahl Cloyd Union was a unique experience. Michael Reineri's introduction and liner notes added a personal touch, while Jimmy Capps' technical expertise ensured a quality recording."

Julian Fowler, Beach Music Historian and collector, said, "The Embers were very lucky in that early in the game they got hooked up with Jimmy Capps and Jimmy Capps Productions. Jimmy had national connections and the first record that the Embers recorded came out on Ace Records, which at that time was a national record label. And from that, The Embers later recorded a number of songs on Jimmy's JCP Records, which have become big collector's items, not only in this country but in Europe as well."

Charlie Brown shares a fond memory: "I remember meeting Bobby, and what he was so excited about was we'd play a song by the Beatles, and then we'd play a song by The Embers. And they thought that was so cool. Anything that lasts over fifty years has to have the ability to adapt to the times. And I think one of the things that's made The Embers popular over all these years is their ability to do that."

Reflecting on their recording sessions, Bobby said, "We spent a lot of time in Jimmy Capps' studio, which was located under a movie theater on Hillsborough Street right across from NC State University. The studio was small, maybe 12' x 12', and the walls were covered with empty egg crates to absorb the sound. Recording at Jimmy Capps Studios was like a dream. We were young and everybody's dream was to record an album. It was a prestige thing. We wanted to make our mark."

Recording at that time was quite the adventure, done on two-track recorders. "If you made a mistake, you had to stop and start over. You had to play a song from start to finish. If there was a mistake, you had to redo the whole thing. You couldn't just stop, fix the mistake, and pick back up where you left off. The whole thing had to be redone in one take."

Despite the challenges, the experience was invaluable. "Recording back then required precision and discipline," Bobby noted. "That process taught us a lot about musicianship and performance. Spending hours in the studio allowed us to hone our skills and experiment with our sound."

Chapter 11

In the fall of 1964, The Embers returned to Jimmy Capps' studio to record their interpretation of Martha Reeves & The Vandellas' "In My Lonely Room," a song that had become a regular part of their sets. The flip side was a cover of James Brown's late 1950s hit "Good Good Lovin'." Released in December 1964 on the JCP label, it received regional airplay on many stations, elevating The Embers to local celebrity status.

The shift in the local radio scene and the strategic partnership with WKIX were monumental for The Embers' growth. The station's influence and the relationships the band built with the DJs were crucial in getting their music heard.

In 1965, Joe Murnick and Jim Crockett, event promoters in the Southeast US, were organizing a major event at Dorton Arena featuring The Beach Boys. The California surf group was huge having recently released "Little Honda" and their most recent smash hit "Help Me Rhonda."

The WKIX "Men of Music" were promoting the show and Charlie Brown suggested that The Embers would be the perfect opening act. Taking Brown's suggestion,

Murnick and Crockett scheduled The Embers to open for the Beach Boys on July 12 at Dorton Arena located on the NC State Fairgrounds.

The Embers were pictured with The Beach Boys on the poster and immediately preceded the featured act. Two other local bands, The Unknown IV and The Inmates, preceded The Embers.

"While other bands came out in tuxedos and black tie," Bobby recalled, "we wore Weejuns, khaki pants, and madras shirts." Before the performance, Bobby met with Joe Murnick at the arena and was introduced to Dick Duryea, the Beach Boys' manager.

"I was a movie buff," Tomlinson admitted, "so I asked him, 'Dick Duryea, are you related to Dan Duryea?' Dan Duryea was a 'heavy' in movies of the day, always playing the villain. Dick smiled and said, 'That's my father.' I was more starstruck by that than meeting The Beach Boys."

Bobby asked Duryea if they could meet The Beach Boys but Duryea was noncommittal. "He looked at me and said, 'I don't know if that'll be possible. They're really busy.' I understood."

When the concert started, The Embers played hits like "Hang On Sloopy" and "Stubborn Kind of Fellow," and finished with "Dixie" energizing the crowd to a fever pitch. "We had people standing on their chairs, screaming," Tomlinson remembered. "The Beach Boys were watching from the side of the stage, giving us thumbs up."

After their set, Tomlinson was surprised to find Dick Duryea waiting at the bottom of the stairs. "Duryea shook my hand and said, 'That was a great show. The Beach Boys want you to come down and visit during intermission. It's Dennis Wilson's birthday.'" Tomlinson couldn't resist a bit of playful irony, responding, "I don't know if we can do that. We're really busy." Duryea did a double take before realizing the jest, saying, "I asked for that, didn't I?"

At The Beach Boys' birthday celebration, Bobby struck up a conversation with Carl Wilson telling him he had a 45-rpm record player in his car, an unusual feature for the time. After the show, "Carl and I met up at their hotel, drove around, and played records. He was impressed by the Southern rhythm & blues I played in my car. He asked what I was doing later and invited me to the Holiday Inn North where they were staying. We became fast friends."

Later on, Carl would record 'What You Do To Me.' Bobby mused, "I like to think maybe I influenced him a bit."

The Embers were booked as part of an Interfraternity Council weekend event featuring The Temptations at a time when the Temptations were hot, hot, hot. Between 1964 and 1965, the Motown recording artists had made themselves at home on Billboard Magazine's Top-40 charts. Their song "My Girl" was on the chart for months, eventually becoming The Temptations' first #1 hit. Other big chart movers at the time included "Girl (Why You Wanna Make Me Blue)," "My Baby," "Get Ready," and "Since I Lost My Baby."

The event was scheduled at Riddick Stadium, the 23,000-seat home of the NC State Wolfpack football team from 1907 through 1965, which was scheduled for demolition after the fall football season. "The contract called for us to be the opening act," said Tomlinson. "Being a top act with major hits, they brought key musicians with them. But some of our band members played with their band," recalled Durwood Martin, keyboardist for The Embers from 1964-1968 and 1970-1976. They had me with my piano and Frank Reich playing sax.

"The stage was a flatbed trailer and The Temptations were doing all their steps and dance movements and the trailer was rocking side to side. Now that was a lot of fun."

In 1965, The Embers recorded and released "Just For The Birds" on the JCP label, marking a pivotal moment in their early career. This LP showcases the band's versatility and mastery of rhythm and blues, with a selection of songs that blend soul, pop, and the beach music sound for which they became known. The record opens with a lively cover of "My Girl Sloopy," which was a huge hit around the same time. The album continues with iconic

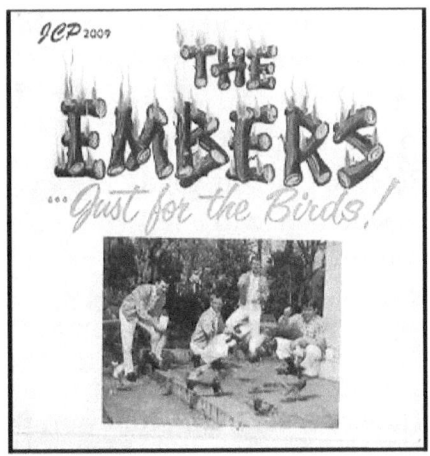

tracks like "Up On The Roof," "I'm On The Outside Looking In," "Irresistible You," "Rockin' Crickets" and "Little Young Lover" and a cover of Curtis Mayfield's "Before Six" which was The Embers Theme song. With a mix of covers and their own instrumental flair, "Just For The Birds" highlights The Embers' growing ability to bridge R&B with the burgeoning beach music scene, cementing their status as one of the genre's foundational bands.

Then on November 10, 1965, the evening air around Reynold's Coliseum in Raleigh was again electric with anticipation. A crowd of 14,000 college and high school students were buzzing with excitement and wonder about what an evening with The Embers, Patti LaBelle and the Bluebelles, The Vibrations, and The Rolling Stones would bring. Mick Jaggar and the band had been to the United States twice in 1964 and were on their second tour in 1965. This night was their first visit to Raleigh.

Durwood Martin recalled the night with a mixture of awe and amusement. "Joe Murnick, the promoter who brought the Stones here, comes and gets us and says, 'Come on, I want you guys to meet The Rolling Stones.'" Durwood recalled, "I can't tell you who was who at that particular time. They looked really grubby and dirty.

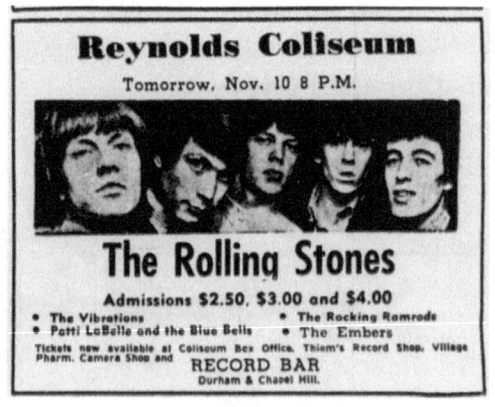

They had very long hair and it was greased down on their heads. They had on leather jackets and were not very friendly. I don't think they meant it, that's just the way it was in their culture. Joe introduced us to them, and they would hardly speak to us. Bobby held out his hand to shake hands with one of them and the man just looked at him and turned his head. Bobby shrugged and said, 'Let's get out of here boys before we catch something.'"

The Embers opened the show followed by The Rolling Stones, who took the stage and played for about fifteen minutes. They were followed by Patti Labelle and the Bluebells, and then The Vibrations.

As the night drew to a close, it was clear that the audience had witnessed more than just a concert. It was a kaleidoscope of musical talent and showmanship. Each act, from the gritty rock of The Rolling Stones to the soulful harmonies of The Embers, Patti LaBelle and the Bluebelles, and the dynamic performances of The Vibrations, had left an indelible mark.

Jim Lewis of the Raleigh News and Observer noted it this way:

> "It was the other acts of the night that truly shone. The Embers, a local band with a growing reputation, took the stage with an electrifying presence. Their performance was seamless, each member perfectly in sync as they delivered soul classics like "Fool in Love," "Stubborn Kind of Fellow," and "Ooh Poo Pah Doo." The pinnacle of their set was "Good All Over," a number that stood out as the evening's highlight, showcasing their vocal prowess and infectious energy."

For The Embers, it was a moment when they stood on the same stage with rock legends and held their own. "We did our thing, and the audience loved it," Bobby reflected. "It was a night to remember, not just for us, but for everyone who was there. Music has a way of bringing people together, and that night, we all shared something special."

CHAPTER 12

IN THE SPRING OF 1965, The Embers embarked on a new venture that would change the landscape of the Carolina music scene. After years of playing countless gigs, particularly those at Jim Thornton's Dance Club, Tomlinson envisioned a club of their own. "We kept playing and playing and our popularity kept growing," he reflects. One day, inspired by Thornton's success, he thought, "If he can do it, we can do it." This belief ignited their entrepreneurial spirit.

Tomlinson found an old warehouse downtown on West Davie Street in Raleigh, North Carolina and contacted its owner, Jillian Rand. Introducing himself as a member of The Embers, he expressed his interest in her warehouse. To his pleasant surprise, Rand was already familiar with the band.

"Oh, I'm very familiar with you boys. You play for a lot of the debutante parties," she remarked.

This recognition further fueled Tomlinson's determination to open a club of their own. After some negotiation, Rand agreed to rent the space for $350 a month. With his father's help, Tomlinson secured the funds.

The warehouse, a vast 8,000 square feet previously used for storing old tires, was daunting. But where others saw dirt and decay, Tomlinson saw potential. "We went in there, and we cleaned it out and started building the club," he recounts. Alongside his father, a versatile craftsman, and Jackie, they built a bar and a stage, installed a suspended ceiling over the bar, and created tiered risers for seating. Jackie led the decorating effort, painting the ceiling black and leaving the brick walls natural. They polished the concrete floor with clear varnish and laid black-and-white checkered tiles near the stage to create a large dance floor. An outdoor dock area was enclosed with a cyclone fence, adding to the club's charm.

As they neared the club's grand opening, a chance encounter at the Blue Tower Restaurant revealed there was undoubtedly a local buzz about their venture. Tomlinson and Jackie were regulars at the restaurant and known for ordering deluxe cheeseburgers, hash browns, and milk. One evening, Jim Thornton, the

local TV celebrity who owned the dance club where they previously played, commented on their plans. "They tell me you boys are opening a nightclub," he said.

Tomlinson confirmed, "Yes sir, downtown by the railroad tracks."

Thornton skeptically replied, "They won't never find y'all," to which Tomlinson optimistically responded, "Well, maybe they will."

Three weeks later, on the grand opening night of their first Embers Club, the band played for a large, enthusiastic, and receptive crowd. As luck would have it, Tomlinson and Thornton met up again at the Blue Tower after the club closed. Tomlinson leaned down to Thornton and whispered, "Jim, six hundred and twenty-nine people found us tonight."

The Embers Club quickly became a popular nightspot, a home away from home. Bobby's mother managed the door while his father ran the club. "It was very successful," Tomlinson notes. "Going to that club was like going home."

The club featured a large dance floor and booked big-name entertainment including such renowned groups as Maurice Williams and the Zodiacs, Chester Mayfield and the Casuals, The Drifters, The Catalinas, The Shirelles, Wilson Pickett, Rufus Thomas, and Archie Bell and The Drells. "We even had Jackie Wilson in there one night, and he drew fourteen hundred people."

"If we didn't have a booking, we'd play there ourselves," Tomlinson explains. "And every time *we* played it packed the house."

Tomlinson recalled the time The Embers backed up Little Anthony and the Imperials there. "We rehearsed with them before the show and Jackie asked Little Anthony if they would do the song 'Reputation' which the Imperials had recorded as the B-side of "Hurt So Bad," Tomlinson said, thinking it would be a good song for The Embers to record. Anthony told him, "I have so many songs running around in my head, I cannot remember all the words."

The Embers recorded both "Hurt So Bad" and "Reputation" on their 1967 LP "Burn You A New One."

Reflecting on the impact of The Embers Club, Tomlinson shares a touching anecdote. "One person told me that he used to go to The Embers Club when he was like sixteen. 'Your daddy would let me in. Occasionally, he would loan me the money and say, have a good time. If I catch you drinking, I'm going to call your mother.'" Bobby laughed, "I'll remember that forever."

Chapter 13

In 1966, THE EMBERS experienced a significant turning point in their career when they met Bert Caudle. Having recently returned to Raleigh after a successful stint as a top executive with Sears Roebuck and Company, Caudle was captivated by the band's potential. After hearing The Embers play a few times, he saw an opportunity to help elevate their career.

Caudle approached The Embers with a thrilling proposition—to transform their appearance and stage presence. "He brought in two entertainment professionals from California who had worked with prominent musicians and stars on the West Coast," recalled Tomlinson. "They re-staged us with the drummer on the left, the horn on the right, and the keyboard player and vocalist-guitarist in the middle. It was a whole new dynamic for us."

Caudle didn't stop at re-staging. He took the band to New York, where he outfitted them with a professional look reminiscent of entertainers in prominent Las Vegas or New York nightclubs. The new wardrobe included coats and ties, suits, and dress shirts with or without ties, depending on the gig. "Bert took us to one of those clothing warehouses and bought us clothes," said Tomlinson. "And these two guys came and staged us and put together a show."

Caudle had new promotional photos taken in these outfits and created new promotional literature using the agency name Talent International Associates. This transformation was unveiled at a showcase in downtown Columbia, South Carolina, a pivotal moment for the band. Several regional booking agents attended, and this exposure opened doors, leading to extended bookings beyond just one weekend or one-time outings.

The Embers

Exclusive Management
Talent International Corporation
Suite 224 York Building Cameron Village
Raleigh, North Carolina

However, 1967 brought a tragic event—Jimmy Capps' untimely death.

This loss prompted The Embers to take control of their destiny by establishing their own record label, Embers Entertainment Enterprises (eEe), named after their club business. This move allowed them to have greater control over their music and to release their work independently. They used the label for most of their single and album releases and even helped other regional artists by releasing their records under the eEe label.

Realizing the potential to streamline their operations and cut out the middleman, The Embers also launched their own booking agency. Initially, they had worked with Ted Hall of Hit Attractions Agency, but his commission ate into their earnings. Bobby explained, "Ted got a percentage of every booking we had. It added up to a lot." Thus, Embers Booking Agency was born, allowing the band to handle bookings directly and retain the commission. "We were popular. We knew so many people. We could book ourselves as well as anybody else."

During this transformative period, The Embers also worked on their third album. They decided to explore a new studio and laid down tracks at Arthur Smith Studio in Charlotte. Arthur Smith's illustrious career as a musician, composer, songwriter, and entertainer made him a pivotal figure in Charlotte's vibrant music scene throughout much of the 20th century. In addition to Smith's own success, his recording studio, Arthur Smith Studio, also played an invaluable role in shaping Charlotte's musical landscape by providing a space for countless other musicians and performers to create and record.

Frank Reich recalled the event. "James Brown had recorded there the night before and he called into the studio while we were recording wanting to know if he could get back in the studio for some more recording time. They told him 'We've got a group here that's recording, so we'll ask them if they'll give you a couple of hours.' So, they came down and asked us, and we said, 'Sure, yeah, James Brown can come here and do some recording, provided we can stay in the room and watch what's going on, because that'll be a learning experience for us.'

"So, sure enough, James Brown comes in and he's bringing all their equipment in and setting up, and we're over there to the side just wide-eyed. They had four horns, two saxes, a trumpet—maybe it was three saxes and a trumpet. We met each of them, then got out of their way.

"I don't think they really knew what they were going to record," Frank mused, "because the guitarist went over to the rhythm section and he was doing this rhythm on his guitar, teaching each one of them what they're going to play, and they're playing riffs. Riffs are where you do the same thing over and over and over. And then he went over to the drummer and the piano man, and he was teaching them.

"Man, this guitar player was good. And the drummer, he fell right into it, and this was starting to really sound good. We were punching each other and in awe of what they were doing. I said, 'Man, this is going to be a hit.' And James went and listened to it in the sound booth, then came in and made some changes.

"They did it all again either twice or three times, then James Brown said, "Okay, that's a rap. That's all we need.' And these guys all packed up and left.

"Then James goes in a little room with a big microphone, and he's listening to it, and getting into it, and there's no music in front of him. And he's holding his belt and doing his feet side to side as he normally does. And he started singing. Well, he started singing words that were completely screw-ball.

"I mean, they didn't make any sense. We were looking at each other and saying, he's making this up as he goes. And he got through with it and went up to the sound room and listened to himself. He came back out and did it again. And I said, 'man, this was a waste of time. You know, all that great music.'

"And here this guy is making all this gibberish. He went and listened to it, came back, and said, 'that's a rap.' And he came over and shook all our hands and said, 'Thanks a whole lot. I really appreciate you sharing the time with us.'

"And then he left. The song was 'Papa's Got a Brand New Bag.' Sold two million copies."

Among the tracks The Embers recorded that night include "It Ain't Necessary" and "Mexican Divorce," released on JCP Records in late 1966. Charlie and the WKIX "Men of Music" gave "It Ain't Necessary" significant airplay. Charlie shared it with his industry contacts, including Elliot Murnick, the son of Joe Murnick, the Raleigh concert promoter. Charlie and Elliot had connections in New York and were instrumental in introducing the band to Bell Records. Although these songs got some airtime in the region, they didn't significantly impact the charts.

Charlie Brown got to know key management at some of the larger record labels, including Jerry Wexler at Atlantic Records. Brown was sharing what songs seemed to be popular in the region and he and Wexler came up with the idea to put together a twelve-song compilation of popular R&B music by Atlantic Records artists. The album was called "Beach Beat" and was promoted as music heard in the summertime, with suds in hand, and enjoyed by young people everywhere on the jukeboxes, but never available in record stores till now.

One of the songs on the LP was Stick McGhee's "Wine Spo-De-O-Dee," Atlantic's first number one R&B smash in 1949. Wexler was interested in the South because, in the early 1950s, he had noticed Atlantic's record "Wine Spo-De-O-Dee" had its most sales and jukebox play along the Carolina Coast. It was enough of a blip that he sent a staffer to investigate the jukebox at Charlie's Place, a Black-owned nightclub near Myrtle Beach. Wexler made note that white kids were learning about Black music at the club, enough so that the region was a hotspot for Atlantic's products.

The album sold well, and Wexler and Brown collaborated on "Beach Beat Vol. 2" in 1968 with Charlie Brown writing the liner notes himself. The two albums included songs by The Drifters, Barbara Lewis, The Coasters, The Clovers, and Willie Tee—basically, they contained the greatest hits of beach music, and several were covered by many bands including some by The Embers.

We believe this connection of Charlie Brown and Jerry Wexler over Southern music was the impetus for Atlantic picking up The Embers' second national release "Where Did I Go Wrong/You Got What I Got." It was released in April 1969.

Nevertheless, The Embers were hard at work on their next album which featured distinctive interpretations of The Temptations' "Get Ready," Willie Tee's "Teasing You," The Radiants' "Ain't No Big Thing," Jerry Butler's "Aware of Love," and Dionne Warwick's "Walk On By." Several of these songs would get second and third lives on other albums or as singles.

Bert Caudle helped with the album cover design and the photos used.

"Burn You A New One" was released in 1967. It was a significant album for The Embers. Several regional record stores and chains included it in their display advertising with national records. Some regional stores held LP signings in their stores. The album sold well.

Meanwhile, despite his good intentions, Caudle's involvement eventually faded, but his influence remained and positively impacted the band's journey. During this time, Charlie Brown at WKIX saw potential in a couple of tunes from the "Burn You A New One" LP. A new 45 featuring 'It Ain't Necessary' and 'Ain't No Big Thing,' came out in March of 1967 on Bell Records. Tomlinson remembered, "Both songs were always well received in our shows. And that's how it came to be. We never got much money, but that was a national label. That was our second national record."

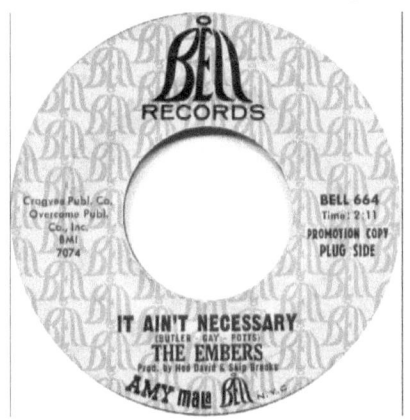

Reflecting on this period, Bobby remarks, "It was a whirlwind time for us. We were recording, performing, and taking control of our destiny. Those days defined The Embers and set us on a path to lasting success."

Chapter 14

IN THE LATE 1960s, The Embers Club in Raleigh thrived as a bustling live music hub. The Embers played often but also brought in other national touring and regional artists, which freed them to play elsewhere. The Eastern coast of NC was a popular destination for them.

Craig Woolard, who would later become lead vocalist and saxophone player with The Embers, shares his childhood memories. "If you lived in Washington, NC, and wanted to go to the beach, you went to Atlantic Beach. And if you went to Atlantic Beach, you went to the Pavilion. We'd go down and sit there and watch those bands and everybody dancing. Because all the really good guys, in the heat of the summer, would have on long-sleeve, heavily starched, powder blue, button-down collar, Gant shirts, starched khakis, and Weejuns with no socks. And they'd get out there and do these great moves and dances, but they never seemed to break a sweat.

"Meanwhile, I would sit there in my shorts and T-shirt, pouring with sweat, watching the bands and wondering how they could do that. I remember thinking, 'Man, if I could get up there on the stage here at Atlantic

Beach, that would be about as close to making it as you could get.'"

The Embers drew huge crowds to the Pavilion for years without demanding a raise. "We were having a ball," Tomlinson said. "And continually gaining in popularity."

Frank Reich, saxophone player for The Embers, added, "A lot of folks would come from all over the eastern part of the state just to see us. And they would party with us, go to dinner with us, and we'd see them during the day. Great place."

As the summer of 1967 waned, a pivotal moment unfolded for The Embers. Tomlinson's bandmates lingered in the parking lot while he entered the Pavilion to collect their pay. Aubrey Mason, the Pavilion owner, lounged at his desk, grinning broadly. Tomlinson recalls, "After a couple of years, we were getting $700 for a Friday night, Saturday night, and a Sunday afternoon, which was a lot of money at the time. But we knew we were doing well. We were outdrawing all the other groups and, just like now, everybody wants more."

Tomlinson, seeking a raise to $1,000 for the weekend, was met with a memorable retort. "He leaned back and looked at me," Tomlinson remembers. "And said, 'Pard (short for partner), hell will freeze over before I pay you $1,000.' At that time, I expected him to negotiate, but that wasn't the case. I walked out and said, 'Boys, I might have screwed up. It looks like we won't be playing here anymore.'"

Undeterred by the rejection, Bobby's unwavering resolve burned within him, fueling his determination to overcome any obstacle. He knew that setbacks were merely stepping stones to success.

As Bobby Tomlinson's hopes for a raise were dashed in the Pavilion, a twist of fate awaited him. As Tomlinson started his car, something unexpected caught his eye. "I turned my headlights on, and the beam shown directly on a sign that said, 'Will build to suit tenant.' I always believed in fate. It was a Raleigh number. I wrote the number down and I drove back home."

The following day, Tomlinson contacted Maynard (Cutie) Mosley, a prominent businessman and pool shark. "He owned a pool room known as The Sphinx Club, on Hillsborough Street adjacent to NC State," Tomlinson said. "He was well-known around the state for his billiard skills. I went to see him and introduced myself. 'I know who you are,' he said. 'My daughter has been to see you guys play quite frequently.'"

When Bobby asked about the beach property, Mosley said, "Tell me what you want and I'll build it."

"We need about 10,000 square feet," Bobby said. "And there's one stipulation. It has to be ready by Easter."

Easter was the unofficial kickoff for the summer season and The Embers traditionally opened that weekend at the Pavilion. Mosley and his team worked tirelessly to meet the deadline, erecting a large, 10,000-square-foot venue along with a surf shop for his son on one end and an upstairs apartment.

As the grand opening on Thursday, April 11, 1968, approached, one critical detail remained—securing a beer license. When the state alcohol official inspected the venue, he informed them that the license process typically took three days. "We need the license tomorrow," Tomlinson said.

The agent shook his head. "I don't know how that can happen."

Undeterred, Tomlinson suggested a solution. "Let me hand deliver it."

The official agreed and at 9 o'clock the next morning, he was at the courthouse in New Bern. He then drove 95 miles south to Wilmington, and then 130 miles to Raleigh, navigating through bureaucratic steps along the way to ensure the club had all necessary permits.

"I called the guys down at the beach from a pay phone in Raleigh and said, 'Get the beer trucks lined up. I'm on the way.' I got to the beach about four o'clock in the afternoon and all the trucks were in line. We put the beer on ice and opened with a bang."

As the sun neared the horizon to the west, casting a warm golden glow on the venue, the sound of crashing waves was blended with the sound of soulful melodies that filled the air.

Jackie Gore remembers that first night, Easter weekend of 1968. "We had them lined up four abreast out the front door all the way up the street trying to get in that place. It was just a wide-open building with a concrete floor.

"We had a row of booths all the way around the inside edge. There was no air conditioning, just ceiling fans that blew hot air around. It was the hottest place you'd ever been. But in those days, we didn't even notice it.

"I probably drank twelve or fifteen beers at night standing on stage, and that's how life was back then. Beer and beach music. And that's kind of how the term beach music came about."

The grand opening on Easter weekend in 1968 was a resounding success. The Showmen came in to join The Embers that Sunday. The new Embers Club, a large, metal building with big ceiling fans and a concrete floor, was packed the entire weekend. "It was wall-to-wall. People were everywhere," Tomlinson recalled.

The Embers Beach Club at Atlantic Beach was a pulsating oasis of music where the crowd's electric energy mingled with the soulful melodies pouring from the stage. The concrete floor reverberated with dancers' rhythmic footsteps as the ceiling fans whirled above.

Despite the lukewarm beer on opening day, the event was a triumph. "The rent for the building was $10,000 a year," Jackie noted, "which was a lot of money in those days. We made enough money that first weekend to almost pay the rent for the first year."

Chapter 15

THE EMBERS BEACH CLUB at Atlantic Beach soon brought in big-time talent, featuring performances by Archie Bell and The Drells, The Tams, The Drifters, Doug Clark and the Hot Nuts, The O'Kaysions, Bob Collins and The Fabulous Five, The Four Tops, Junior Walker and The All Stars, and Billy Joe Royal among others. And, of course, The Embers were frequently on the billing.

Frank Reich, saxophonist for The Embers recalled, "We would play there a week at a time and invariably it would be with another group, especially on Friday and Saturday nights. We would play, like, with The Tams. The Tams would play for an hour and we would play for an hour. And that place was not air-conditioned. It was hot and we were dripping wet after every set."

Tommy "T-Bird" Smith, syndicated beach music radio DJ, put it this way. "It was hot. It was sticky. And it was packed. You were elbow to elbow. And I loved it."

Keith Houston of KHP Records and the Band of Oz recalled, "When you walked up to the door you could smell it and you could hear the music coming out. And it was always jammed, never a small crowd, always a huge crowd. We would go in there and open up for some of the large acts. Opened up for Jackie Wilson one time and it was just a tremendous party."

J.D. Cash, recording artist, promoter, and former lead singer for Bob Kuban and the In Men, recalled, "Every Labor Day they would do a marathon because back in those days the beach rolled up the carpet after Labor Day. And they would hire four bands. I was fortunate enough to play it for two years. And it was the most fun. It would always have The Embers. And my first year, it also included my band The Castaways, Gene Barber and the Cavaliers, and The Four Tops. We'd start at noon and alternate every hour until midnight. And those were just memorable great times."

Meanwhile, Aubrey Mason's refusal to grant The Embers a well-deserved raise proved to be a fatal mistake for the Pavilion. "The pavilion went out of business the next year," Tomlinson reflects.

In 1968, The Embers shared the stage with Archie Bell and The Drells and soon added Archie's chart-topping hit "Tighten Up" to their setlist. And, according to Bobby, while playing it one night at The Embers Beach Club in Atlantic Beach, Jackie got into a groove and, out of nowhere, seamlessly blended in "Far Away Places," a nostalgic tune from the late 1940s that fit the music well. Originally performed by artists like Bing Crosby, Perry Como, and dozens of other artists, the song captured a yearning for distant lands.

Gore's version, however, carried a deeper weight at the time as the Vietnam War raged. It was a "faraway place with strange-sounding names." With its dreamy melody reimagined, Gore infused the track with a new energy and poignant emotion that resonated with audiences.

Realizing the potential for the song, The Embers went to work and refined it, coming up with a creative arrangement. Soon, the song became a mainstay in their setlists.

Romeo Davis and Jerry Goodman, representatives of Charlotte's Mangold-Bertos record distributors happened to be in the Raleigh Embers Club one night when The Embers performed the song. Dick Allen, a Los Angeles-based talent manager, who was with MCA at the time was with Davis and Goodman. Among Allen's clients were Chuck Berry, Little Richard, and James Brown. Allen loved The Embers' arrangement and inquired if they would mind if he shopped the song with some acquaintances. The Embers had recorded a live raw demo recently and Allen took the tape with him to California.

A few weeks later, Allen called Tomlinson and said his friend Mike Curb liked the song. Curb was President of MGM Records. "They're interested," Allen said. "But he asked me if we had any objections to them recording the rhythm track out there and bringing it here and letting us sing it." And I said, 'No, we don't have any objections.' So, they recorded the music and sent it back.

By early 1970, Joe Saraceno and Mike Gordon, two of Curb's trusted producers, were back in Raleigh with the music bed. "We were all astounded by who was playing on it," Tomlinson said. The Embers went to the studio and recorded the vocals. The track was mixed. The flip side was an up-tempo, contemporary number titled "Watch Out Girl."

By the summer of 1970, when MGM released the record, "Far Away Places" would become The Embers' biggest hit, solidifying its place as a classic in their repertoire. It got airplay in many major markets, but sadly, MGM fired Mike Curb, and the promotion budget for the record went with him.

Despite the setback, the record captured hearts and minds in the South. Chris Beachley mentioned The Embers' "Far Away Places" in one of his "Rare Beach Sounds" features in a 1979 issue of *It Will Stand* magazine. "The Embers' biggest chance for success came with their 1970 tune they recorded for MGM. The flip side, 'Watch Out Girl,' is hot in England's disco clubs."

"Far Away Places" ranks high on some notable All-Time Favorite charts. John Hook ranked the song #1 for his 1971 Year-End Top 20. Chris Beachley and Hook ranked it #18 in their first All-Time Top 50 Beach Music Chart compiled in 1982. In 2007, Hook and Christopher Biehler listed "Far Away Places" at #21 on their *The Beach Music & Shag All Time Top 200*.

Dr. Rick Simmons included it as one of two songs by The Embers in his 2018 *Carolina Beach Music Encyclopedia*. "Though it was well-known at the time, setting it to that 'Tighten Up' beat, allowed The Embers — now consisting of John Thompson, Durwood Martin,

Johnny Hopkins, Ray Rivera, Bobby Tomlinson, and Jackie Gore—to make it their own and soon they were playing it for audiences throughout the area."

Mark Black, a future member of The Embers, said, "I think "Far Away Places" set the standard for beach music, and when the term Beach Music came around was about the same time. And I think that kind of solidified what beach music is."

"In 1968, Durwood Martin got drafted," reported John Thompson. "But he didn't bother to tell anybody he'd been drafted. So, at the last minute, Bobby called me. You remember, at that time there were only four Embers—Bobby, Jackie, Frank, and Durwood. They didn't have a bass player, Durwood played bass on a bass piano. So, Bobby Tomlinson called me and wanted me to go sit in for him one night in Kinston to play and sing at the Kinston Country Club.

"So, I went, played, and sang a few songs. When it was over, Jackie Gore walked up to me and said, 'You going to stay with us?' And I said, 'Well, no. I got my own band, a group out of Burlington called The Monzas.' And from that day forward, Bobby Tomlinson called me like every day for two weeks and he kept showing up in

Cadillacs and Corvettes and I'm thinking 'Wait a minute, I ain't driving no Cadillac or Corvette. What's wrong?'

"Anyway, they offered me

more money than I'd ever seen, so I went. And that was the beginning. And I stayed with them, I think, I was with them for ten years. And, boy, let me tell you, we had a time. We had a big time."

In the late 1960s, Ted Hall of Hit Attractions in Charlotte offered The Embers a chance to step into concert promotion. Hall's firm had secured several big-name R&B recording artists on seven to fourteen-day contracts at set prices. He proposed a profit-sharing arrangement for a series of Raleigh's Memorial Auditorium shows.

The Embers would handle groundwork, distribute posters, partner with local sponsors, and prep the facility. On show days, they would open the concert and sometimes provide backup for other acts. Between 1968 and 1969, The Embers shared the stage with stars like Jerry Butler, The Intruders, Jackie Wilson, Sam and Dave, and Dionne Warwick.

Bobby vividly remembers meeting The Dells, who were at their peak. "Their contract included a special provision rider—their dressing room was required to have a case of Black Jack Daniels on hand," he recalls. Despite the glamorous business, their foray into concert promotion had challenges, including a costly venture with Sonny & Cher.

These experiences marked The Embers' adventurous foray into concert promotion, filled with highs and lows, memorable performances, and invaluable lessons.

In the late 1960s, The Embers were well-known for not just their musical talent but also their playful, and at times, reckless antics on the road. While fans saw a polished performance on stage, life behind the scenes was often far more chaotic and humorous. One such story, involving fireworks and a near disaster, has become legendary among the band members. It starts with John Thompson and Frank Reich reminiscing about a wild night on the road that could have ended very differently.

"We had gotten into this fireworks phase of our life," laughed John Thompson. "Everybody would see where they could buy the most powerful fireworks. Well, I bought some Roman candles and we were always riding down the road lighting cherry bombs, throwing them out at each other, and driving over them. Well, I had the Roman candles, and here comes Frank Reich and Jackie Gore in the van pulling up beside Bobby's Eldorado, and I lit that thing and I stuck it out of the window."

Frank added, "We were side-by-side going down the highway. Jackie Gore was driving and John Thompson's firing Roman candles at us. So, by God, I went in the back of the van and I got ours."

John said, "And Jackie had just rolled the window down on the van to yell something at Bobby and I."

Frank added, "So here we were firing Roman candles at each other going down the highway side-by-side."

John breaks in, "Well, I shot one and it went right across Jackie's eyebrows."

Frank said, "Jackie threw his head back—"

John interrupts, "—and hit his head on the air conditioning unit. Knocked him out. Now remember, he's driving the van. Well, it lit up the whole inside of the van."

Frank continued, "I said, 'Jackie, are you alright?' Well, he's starting to slump over and I'm grabbing the wheel."

John continued the story, "Frank's trying to drive and stomp out this ball that was on fire at his feet, and still the Roman candles in *his* hand keep firing. You can't cut them off. He had to keep it pointed out the window and empty the thing while driving the van and trying to stomp out the fire."

"I'm holding on to the steering wheel," Frank explained, "and I'm slapping Jackie on top of the head, 'Wake up, wake up!'" Frank sighed. "He finally came to and we were okay."

John shook his head and chuckled, "You know, between all of us, I swear it's a wonder we're alive."

Chapter 16

As the 1970s dawned, The Embers were enjoying more attention than usual. They had the two Embers Clubs operating, one in downtown Raleigh and one at Atlantic Beach. They found large receptive crowds whenever they played. They also were keeping their fingers crossed that something big was on the horizon. MGM Records executives were working with their rendition of "Far Away Places," the song Jackie Gore added to a cover of Archie Bell and The Drells' "Tighten Up".

The Embers brand was well established and their music, style, and business ventures reflected a deep understanding of their audience and a commitment to excellence. "Far Away Places" served as the perfect anthem for this new decade, a song that celebrated the past while looking forward to the future. With their sights set on new horizons, The Embers were ready to make the 1970s their own, continuing to shape the sound and culture of beach music for years to come.

Then tragedy struck.

Around 4 a.m. on June 8, 1970, The Embers Club on Davie Street caught fire and the entire front half of the structure was gutted. The Fire Marshal reported that the fire was of electrical origin. Among the losses, forty cases of beer were destroyed.

The News and Observer in Raleigh reported it this way:

Club Here Destroyed By Fire

The Embers Club on Davie Street downtown here burned early Sunday. There was no damage estimate available. Bobby Tomlinson, a member of The Embers, the band that owns the club. said late Sunday the fire apparently started in the kitchen or dressing room in the front part of the building and was of electrical origin. He said it was just too early to make an accurate estimate of the damage.

The Raleigh Fire Department answered the call at 4:03 a.m. Sunday and fought the fire for more than two hours.

Tomlinson said the entire front half of the club was gutted. He said the front part of the roof will probably have to be replaced as well as several appliances and fixtures inside.

An ice machine, a draft beer box, the cash register, part of the bar, and more than forty cases of beer were destroyed. "The cash register alone cost about $1500," Tomlinson said. The rug on the stage and a gas heater were also destroyed. The smoke damage was quite heavy.

Tomlinson said several members of his family were in the club looking things over Sunday afternoon when a sofa in the back smoldered and caught fire again. The fire department had to be called again.

Damage to the club was extensive and required months to restore. One humorous note—Wadsworth

Wrecking Company of Raleigh was hired to clear the debris for the reconstruction. They ran an advertisement in the June 27, 1970, Raleigh News and Observer that said "We are now removing the charred embers from The Embers Club...Smoke That Over."

The Embers Club on Davie Street had its "Grand Re-opening" on Saturday, September 19. The Embers played it. Advertising for the event mentioned 'hear The Embers performing their new "hit" record, "Far Away Places." The club returned to normal operations the next week. The new 45 had just been released by MGM Records.

In 1972, Bobby Tomlinson was approached by John O.D. Williams, a prominent real estate developer in Raleigh, and Bill "Puss" Jenkins with a proposal to open a new Embers Club right off Wake Forest Road on Creekside Drive, a prime piece of property owned by Williams.

"They told me to design what I wanted and they would build it, so we built a fantastic club, a show club," Tomlinson said. "The interior was a spectacle of color and luxury, with purple carpets, purple walls, and red furniture. The bartenders and other male staff members were all in tuxedos.

"The stage was built for musicians—an engineering marvel," he said. "It featured two levels and a hydraulic mechanism that extended the second from underneath the main stage, out over the dance floor for floorshows that were now part of The Embers experience.

"It had a great sound system and lighting that was a show in itself," Tomlinson remembered.

The club was designed to rival the grandeur of Las Vegas venues complete with a next-door restaurant serving light snacks and hors d'oeuvres.

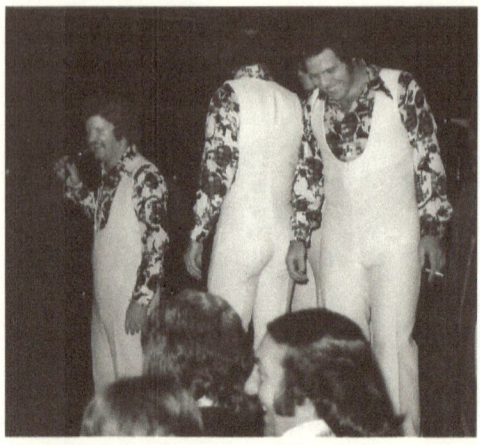

Fashion at the time was as bold as the club's décor. The Embers' attire included leisure suits with bell-bottom pants and sequined shirts with wide collars. The large dance floor was often packed with similarly dressed patrons, bathed in colorful lights that created a memorable visual spectacle.

The Creekside Embers Club opened in 1973 and quickly became a hotspot for great entertainment. While

The Embers played frequently, they shared the stage with

top-name acts such as The Coasters, Fats Domino, Cortez Greer, Clarence Carter, The Tams, The Platters, Little Anthony, Jackie Wilson, Sonny Turner and Sound Limited, and Archie Bell and The Drells. "It was a great club with something going on every night of the week," Tomlinson said.

In addition to the live music, the club featured pool tables, foosball, pinball, and other electronic games. A VIP membership card, sold for $25 a year, offered free admission on Monday and Thursday nights. Friday was "T-G-I-F" happy hour from 5 to 7 for the VIP membership with heavy hors d'oeuvres making it an attractive deal for regular patrons. The Creekside Embers Club was a tremendous success and was "the place to be" in the early to mid-1970s.

The societal changes that began in the late '60s, with longer hair, more profound songs, and heavier music, were shaking the Carolina Beach Music Scene. The college and club scenes changed as audiences demanded more Southern rock and funkier music. Beach music bands began including other genres in their setlists, such as southern rock, R&B funk, and heavier music reminiscent of Chicago, Blood, Sweat & Tears, and Janis Joplin.

After keeping The Embers Club at Atlantic Beach packed for four years, they sold it in 1972. Bobby explained, "The whole music thing changed and we were getting more and more hippies, and all of a sudden, a lot of these people that used to drink beer and dance to beach music were smoking marijuana and doing drugs."

Tomlinson noted that lots of these groups started dressing differently with everyone wearing their hair longer and dressing in leather. Many bands were changing their names as some members of The Embers wanted. But Bobby refused saying, "We're going to stay with what brought us here." The Embers kept doing what they were doing while others changed their music and moved away from beach music. Bobby credits this as a key reason they survived while most others did not.

In the early 1970s, Bobby was persuaded to take a vacation in Atlanta by a lady he'd been dating who had recently moved there from Raleigh. They would talk on the phone all the time, and she wanted him to come down to see this band that was playing in Underground Atlanta, a large-scale entertainment district that had sprouted in the downtown area. The band called themselves The Fabulous Entertainers.

They were a nine-piece showband from Tampa playing at Scarlett O'Hara's, a popular nightspot in Underground Atlanta. They were strong musicians, often playing multiple instruments throughout an evening's performance, and each member fronted the band at some point. In addition to their music and songs, they had routines and skits imitating famous entertainers such as

Moms Mabley, Louis Armstrong, and Frank Sinatra. They also had choreographed dance steps and lots of comedy in between. The Hugh Rodgers Agency managed the band and had booked them throughout the country, including six-week stints in Reno and Las Vegas.

When Bobby saw them perform, he was blown away. "When they hit the stage, my jaw hit the floor. I left there in awe," he said.

Bobby had met the manager of The Fabulous Entertainers, Hugh Rodgers, back in 1963 when The Embers' attorney sent Rodgers a "cease and desist" letter over Rodgers' Washington, D.C. band's name—Little Hugh and The Embers. Bobby's NC Embers had copyrighted the name, so Rodgers' band became known as The Mad Men. Rodgers later started a Talent and Booking Agency in Atlanta in 1968, becoming nationally known by the early 70s.

Before leaving Atlanta, Bobby spoke with Hugh Rodgers and was told that floorshows were the new "in" thing in resorts and big nightclub settings.

At their first rehearsal after Bobby returned to Raleigh, he told the band, "Guys, I've seen the most incredible performance. This band knocked me out of my socks and we've got to do what they're doing. We've got to do floorshows."

The Embers called Fred Little, a musician from Pittsburgh who had moved to North Carolina and had experience with northern bands that performed floorshows and helped The Embers design their first show. It included various acts like The Supremes, James Brown, and a Louis Armstrong impression by Buck Keener who, along with Johnny Hopkins, was one of the trumpeters for the band at the time. They ended their show with "Try A Little Tenderness," starting low and building to a fast, furious, and wild finish.

"At the end of it," Bobby reminisced, "we're going to go bump, bump, bump, loud drum sounds fill the air. And then, we kick the drums over and kick everything over on the floor, take a bow, and walk off the stage. That was our first show."

Soon, The Embers migrated from various song to extended arrangements of medleys into their live performances. The medleys featured major hit songs by some of music's biggest stars, including The Temptations, Junior Walker and The All Stars, and Jackie Wilson. These performances weren't just about faithfully recreating the music—they also included early forays into comedy. The Embers would dress up and mimic the appearance and mannerisms of the artists they were covering, adding a playful, comedic element to their shows. While the comedy was a lighthearted touch, the real focus remained on delivering great music, showcasing the band's ability to honor these iconic hits while engaging and entertaining their audiences. That would change later on.

The performances were a hit, creating a buzz that rippled through the Carolinas. Sensing the momentum, Bobby wasted no time. He picked up the phone and called Rodgers, urging him to see the band live. After witnessing the magic firsthand, Rodgers agreed without hesitation—The Embers were ready for the next level.

Chapter 17

HUGH RODGERS staged an Atlanta Showcase at Uncle Sams, a large, famous nightclub just off Peachtree Street. About thirty club owners were there to see a number of bands perform. The Embers put on a short, well-received show. As a result, the band was soon playing all over the Southeast. They played Miami, Orlando, Palm Beach, Savannah, Lake Pontchartrain, New Orleans, and even spots in Texas and a week-long engagement in Canada.

One booking in St. Petersburg, Florida led to a new helpful connection. Michael Braun, a clothing designer in Tampa Bay who had outfitted stars like Jimi Hendrix, approached Bobby one night after a performance. He said, "You need to come by my shop. I make clothes for big stars, bands, and lots of famous people."

Visiting Michael's sewing shop was an experience. "He made all the clothes for football players because they couldn't get clothes to fit. He also made clothes for lots of other entertainers. Of course, we liked what we saw and asked them to make some outfits for us. Michael and Tony Designs made our fancy clothes, which set us apart. We wore them for years, and nobody knew where they were coming from until Johnny Barker joined us and the secret got out."

Before meeting Michael, The Embers had their outfits made by a local tailor on Hillsborough Street. Bobby always insisted on the band dressing alike to present themselves as a unit. "We had chartreuse green sport coats and matching shoes from a shop on South Wilmington Street. We wore those with white pants and scarves around our necks. Dressing alike became part of our identity."

These new outfits were unique in many ways. Made out of a stretch-knit type material, they wouldn't wrinkle. There were no pockets, except for a small slit pocket like a watch pocket where you could put your key so you wouldn't lose it. Instead of the leg seams being on the outside and inside, they were in the middle, in the front and the back, so they always had a crease. "They never wrinkled," Bobby said.

At that time, the style was bell bottoms with no belts. They had a waistband sewn around the top, making them fit perfectly. "I think the first thing we bought was a pair of jeans. They were faded, but they had buttons all the way down the outside, which could actually be unbuttoned," Bobby recalled.

They ended up with five different outfits. One memorable set included those jeans paired with a yellow shirt. "The shirts didn't have cuffs on them. They buttoned up the front, had collars, and were like a jersey, coming down to your waist. It was probably the best outfit we ever had."

"Our favorite outfit is one we called 'Ribbons.' The outfit had pants with the seams and ribbons making the patterns, and they had French cuffs and buttons. I had a red one, Jackie had black, Gerald had purple. Everybody had a different color. What Michael Braun made for us, nobody else had. When we brought that stuff out in North Carolina, everybody was like, 'Wow!' It was another one of those things that set us apart."

Michael was efficient. He flew with all his clothes in a duffel bag, which Bobby initially thought would wrinkle everything. "Craig had a habit of throwing his clothes in the corner. I always hung everything up, but with these clothes, it honestly didn't matter and they wouldn't wrinkle. I've still got some of those outfits," Bobby said. Some of the shirts were silky, jersey material. Later on, Michael started making outfits with stretch pants. "When you put those on, they fit so well," Bobby added.

When The Fabulous Entertainers split up in March 1972, two members, including singer-bass player Larry Haywood, joined Cortez Greer, a popular nightclub-style singer in Underground Atlanta. Greer and his band often played at the Creekside Embers Club in Raleigh where Bobby and the gang got to know Haywood and invited him to join The Embers in the mid-70s. "Haywood was a ball of fire, a real showman," Bobby mused. "He would run through the crowd and slide on the floor and the crowd loved it."

John Thompson, the bass player for The Embers, sized it up this way. "When we first started doing it, we were like fish out of water. Before the shows, all we ever did was stand there and move around a little while we played. But when we started doing floorshows, we brought in choreographers and bought all these new clothes from Michael and Tony down in Florida."

When the floorshows became a thing, as The Embers would go to a break, they would announce, "We're having a floorshow tonight," and the audience would eagerly arrange their chairs to face the stage so they could see better.

Charlie Brown of WKIX fame said "Their shows were much more than just dancing. They were real shows."

"There was a formula we had," explained Craig Woolard. "We'd do an intro followed by a group song, then usually Jackie would sing a song, and then we'd go into our theme.

In 1976 when Craig, Gerald, and Doug Strange came aboard, The Embers took floor shows to an entirely new level. They developed the "Las Vegas Review," the "Midnight Special," and "Rock and Roll Heaven." Soon they had five floor shows with the addition of "Far Away Places" and "Las Vegas II," a  spin-off of the Las Vegas Review but with other "stars."

"Johnny Hopkins, who everyone loved, was their straight guy and would act as the MC, introducing various acts—band members impersonating famous artists. Jackie did Curtis Mayfield, Craig did Junior Walker, Ray Charles, and Willie Nelson. And, of course, everyone loved Jackie's Raymond Massey skit."

Raymond Massey would make a dramatic entrance  telling jokes and stirring up trouble. "My job usually was to stay on the drums and keep the music going for the others," Bobby said. "But I also played characters, like the Big Bopper in 'Rock and Roll Heaven,' coming out from behind the drums with an enormous cowboy hat to sing 'Chantilly Lace.'"

Another memorable skit was "Having My Baby." Jackie would sing Paul Anka's song by that name while Big John would come out dressed up like an old pregnant woman with a blonde wig and high heels. John would then go into labor and Buck Keener would come out in a diaper and baby hat and jump onto Jackie.

Everybody had a character. Durwood played Elton John, complete with platform shoes, sparkly glasses, and a piano. They even acted out Marty Robbins' song "El Paso," with Bobby as the handsome young cowboy, Durwood as the bad guy, and Buck as Felina. "We entertained each other, and whatever made us laugh usually made the audience laugh too," Thompson added.

Anyone seeing The Embers live with their skits in the '70s or '80s often talks about the unforgettable character Raymond Massey. After a break, Jackie would sneak in the back of the crowd in this redneck persona, donning overalls, a plaid shirt, a metal hard hat, and carrying a beat-up black lunchbox. Raymond Massey would crash their concerts, entering through the crowd and hurling insults at the band, much to the audience's delight.

As Raymond Massey, Jackie would create havoc, tearing through the audience, disrupting the show, and insulting the band. He would meander through the crowd eventually ending up directly in front of the stage. The spotlight would illuminate him, and someone from the band would call out, inviting him to join them on stage.

Jackie, in character, would flip them off, a gesture that never failed to send the crowd into hysterics. When asked his name, he would proudly declare, "My damn name is Massey, Raymond Massey," often claiming to be from a small, recognizable town near their performance venue.

Raymond's antics were legendary. His act was so popular that contracts for their gigs sometimes included a clause insisting on Raymond Massey's presence. In one particularly memorable part of the show, Raymond would "help" the band out of a rut by singing his cover of Sammy Davis, Jr.'s "I've Got To Be Me." And while singing along with the band, he'd slowly strip down to a woman's two-piece bathing suit, complete with a wig and high-heeled shoes. The crowd adored him, and women would often rush the stage to get closer.

Buzz Bolick, former manager of The Treehouse in Charlotte and several clubs in North Myrtle Beach, said, "We had to actually pull ladies off of Jackie while he was on stage. They just loved Raymond Massey."

Bobby recalled a night in Statesville, North Carolina, when Johnny Hopkins was delivering his rehearsed monologue in the lead-up to Raymond's appearance expecting Jackie to appear at any moment in character. But there was no Jackie. Johnny kept talking, growing increasingly desperate until a bandmate informed him that Jackie wasn't coming. They had to improvise another skit to cover the gap. Jackie, in full Raymond attire, had joked with two working policemen saying, "You didn't come here to arrest me did you?" placing an arm on one of the officer's shoulders. The officer did not realize he was with the band, misunderstood the joke, and arrested him for assault.

The band watched in disbelief as Jackie, still in character, was placed in a police car. When Bobby tried to explain it was all part of the show, one of the officers threatened to arrest him too.

Craig Woolard joked, "I hope they strip search him and he has to strip down to that bikini under his overalls."

Chapter 18

ONE OF THE TURNING POINTS for The Embers in the 1970s was their partnership with The Landmark Resort Hotel in Myrtle Beach. In 1973, a majestic, fourteen-story towering hotel went up right in the heart of the Grand Strand. As it was nearing completion, Ralph Johnson, a seasoned lifeguard and bartender, saw an opportunity for more money and applied for and got the job of assistant nightclub manager.

Ralph recalled, "We opened with the New Century Platters and you've never seen so many people in your life. We were the newest, the hottest, the greatest thing to hit Myrtle Beach. So, we had the Platters for two weeks, and we just knocked them dead. You couldn't even get in the hotel. Then, when the Platters left, I went in to work the next Monday to find out they'd fired the nightclub manager and gave his job to me."

During that first year, it didn't take long for Ralph to become the key figure in transforming the resort's Coquina Club into a premier venue. But when he started planning for the spring of '74, Ralph asked himself, "If I was coming down here, who would I want to see?"

And his answer was, "I'd want to see The Embers. So, I contacted The Landmark's booking agent, Don Perry, in Fayetteville, NC, and asked him to see if he could get The Embers for a week down here. Of course, I had to argue with management—that was a lot of money to have The Embers for a week." Johnson continued, "Anyway, we had them for a week, and it was phenomenal!"

By Saturday of Mother's Day weekend, Coquina Club at The Landmark had done so much business, that Johnson decided to move the entire band out on the pool deck overlooking the beach. The Embers started at 1:00 in the afternoon and played an hour and a half. Johnson recalled, "People were coming from the beach, they were coming from the parking lots, they were coming out of the hotel, they were coming from everywhere—just from spreading by word of mouth. And we had so many people out there on the ocean that the Beach Patrol had to come down and monitor the situation. It was just too many people.

"We normally opened the club at 7:30 on Saturdays and closed at midnight. But, needless to say by 6 o'clock that evening, they were lined up all the way down the hall and around the corner, so we had to open the club early just to get them in there."

"And I kept The Embers on stage all night long, just as much as I could keep them on stage. And, I mean, that was the beginning of a long and wonderful partnership, relationship, friendship, whatever you want to name it, between The Embers, myself, and the nightclub business in Myrtle Beach."

The Embers would headline the Coquina Club at the Landmark for almost ten years. Their appearances were week-long stays beginning Easter Weekend and mostly around holiday weeks during the summer through Labor Day. People would book their trips to Myrtle Beach around when The Embers were playing. It became legendary.

Ralph Johnson recalls a story that happened at the Landmark in the mid-70s. "Jackie Gore was into gymnastics at one time, doing flips and karate during the shows. We had booths down the middle of the club where the audience sat and Jackie started walking on the back of one of these rows of booths doing back flips off the booths right out into the middle of the aisle. It was a big central aisle, so we knew he had plenty of room. And he got good at it.

"One night, Jackie was doing his thing and just had them rolling in the aisles. He was walking down the back of the booths and came right to where he was going to do his backflip. So, he caught his breath, turned around, and did a backflip. But he went too far. He hit the booth across the aisle, which was loaded with six people and a table full of drinks.

"He came flying over and landed on the table right in the middle of them. His feet in the air and he ain't missed a note, still singing as hard as he can. Then rolled off the table, stood up, and went back to the middle of the stage. Never missed a beat, just like it was part of the show. And I mean, the people were howling. They were screaming. The people he fell on—it made their night. They were part of The Embers show!"

The partnership with The Landmark Resort Hotel not only helped reintroduce beach music to a new generation but also solidified The Embers' place in the music scene of the 1970s. The Landmark became a hotspot for beach music lovers, and their performances there were a significant part of keeping the genre alive in the 70s.

All the while, The Embers continued to play their Creekside club and other bookings. But as 1976 dawned, the Creekside club would soon be winding down, but there was something new on the horizon.

The Embers toured Florida a lot in the 1970s thanks to their ties to The Hugh Rodgers Agency and the Atlanta Showcase. One of the bookings out of it was an introduction to the Center Court Lounge at The Americana Garden Apartments in Orlando. This large apartment complex, boasting over six hundred apartments and a racquet club with approximately twenty tennis courts, also featured a club that regularly hosted live entertainment.

At the time, The Embers consisted of Bobby, Jackie, Johnny Hopkins, Durwood Martin, Big John Thompson, and Buck Keener. The band had adopted a distinctive style, wearing clothes designed by Michael and Tony, which became part of their unique stage presence. The Americana Garden Apartments complex,  owned by Harrods in Las Vegas, embraced their performances warmly. "They really liked us," Tomlinson recalled, "we packed that place out." As part of their contract, the management provided them with several apartments to stay in during their gigs.

After two strong outings, the complex manager approached Bobby with the idea of recording a live album at the lounge. The complex was willing to cover the expenses, and arrangements were made with a recording company named Full Sail, who brought in all the necessary recording gear.

The Embers' live performance was recorded with plans for a subsequent record release party to be held on-site at the club in the next engagement. However, upon returning to Raleigh, Bobby was surprised with shocking news from Durwood who stated that he, along with Big John Thompson and Buck Keener, had decided to leave The Embers to start their own band, "Hip Pocket."

Bobby was shocked. "You've got to be kidding me. How could you let those guys spend that money? The album will be obsolete before it's even released."

Despite this initial setback, the album took on an unexpected significance over time. It became a sought-after collector's item. John Hook, the well-known beach music historian, highlighted a historical aspect of the album. "The Embers were the first band to use the term 'beach music' in an album.

"Jackie, during the performance, introduced a couple of songs with the phrase, 'We're going to do some music that we call beach music' as the introduction to a two-song medley of 'Green Eyes' and '60-Minute Man.'"

Reflecting on the events later, Tomlinson realized the importance of that album, not just for the music but for the legacy it carried. The Embers had inadvertently coined the term "beach Music" in a recording that would define the genre. The live recording, though initially marred by the departure of key members of the band not only captured the essence of their live performances but now stands as a footnote in beach music history.

The Embers' experience at The Americana Garden Apartments' Center Court Lounge was a blend of success, unexpected challenges, and lasting impact.

CHAPTER 19

WITH THE DEPARTURE of Durwood Martin, Buck Keener, and Big John Thompson in 1976, folks thought The Embers had suffered a major setback. So, Bobby, Jackie, and Johnny Hopkins started looking for replacements and one of the first calls was to Craig Woolard.

On several previous occasions, The Embers had inquired with Craig about joining their band, but it was never a good time for Craig. They hoped this time would be different. They asked around and learned Craig was playing at the Metro Club in Columbia, South Carolina, and called the club.

The way Craig remembers it, "We were rehearsing and the bartender brought me the phone and it was Jackie Gore. I asked what he wanted and he said, 'I want to offer you a job.' And I said, 'Wow, man!' And then he said, 'Actually, I want to offer both you and Gerald a job.' I told Jackie I'd have to call him back.

"After hanging up, I told the guys that Gerald and I had just been offered a job with The Embers, which pretty well decimated rehearsal. I had joined that band because of Gerald Davis. And Gerald had come to me just the week before and told me that if we don't start getting more work around home, which was right outside Goldsboro, he said, 'I'm going to have to leave the band and go back to farming because I've got to be around my family.'

"And I told him, 'If you leave, I don't know what I'm going to do because you're the reason I joined this band.' I told him I'd see what I could do. Then a week later, Jackie called back. So, I knew that joining The Embers was going to be a good thing because it would keep Gerald in music and get him a regular job. So, Gerald and I came in along with Doug Strange, who I had worked with in the Holiday Inn band, and we became 'The New Embers.'"

The Embers had been given the death sentence a few times previously, but it seemed to many that when Durwood Martin, Big John Thompson, and Buck Keener left, it would never be the same. And rightfully so, because Big John had one of the best voices—a powerful, masculine bass who could also sing up high. Durwood Martin was an amazing keyboard player who played with style, and Buck Keener was a wonderful trumpet player and the comedian of the band. So, they were losing an awful lot.

Along with Bobby Tomlinson, Jackie Gore, and Johnny Hopkins, The Embers had a new lineup—Gerald Davis on bass, Doug Strange on keyboard, and Craig Woolard on saxophone and vocals.

Craig reminisced, "We came in from the outside, into a well-known musical entity. Bobby, Jackie, and Johnny had been there for years and were used to how things went for The Embers. For them, it was the same old, same old. But to Gerald and I, it was new, and it was great. I mean, after we joined The Embers, I had people coming up to me raving about something I'd done. It was the same thing I'd been doing for years, it's just that now I was doing it as a member of The Embers."

Gerald remembered, "60-Minute Man was like the number one beach song ever. Big John Thompson had made that song his, but when he left with Durwood and Buck, it was dumped into my lap. So, I started singing it and I've been singing it ever since."

Years later, Craig said, "If I had not been in The Embers, I don't know if I would have remained in music my whole life like I have. I probably would have, but there's a chance that I wouldn't have.

"But being with the Embers changed my life in that I made enough money to have a family. I came from a place where musicians were a breed apart. They were outlaws. That's the way I felt. And when I joined The Embers, here are all these guys with families, houses, mortgages, and car payments. *Are you kidding me?* They're real people, was the way I thought. And I don't know that I would have seen that that is a good way to go had it not been for my career with The Embers."

Chapter 20

As the mid-70s sped by, beach music was in a bit of the doldrums. Disco, southern rock, and funk now created the vibe in many nightclubs and concerts. But The Embers were still kicking, thanks to their involvement in a new club in town.

Hilton Hotels had recently purchased some existing hotels in the Raleigh area and Jim Mieler, who managed one of the hotels, called Bobby and had him go over one morning. He told Bobby, "I think if we could put The Embers in here, we could get a crowd and create more occupancy."

The club was actually located underground, down a flight of stairs in the hotel basement. When you entered the club, the raised stage was in a corner on the left. The back wall of the stage was a collage of tiny mirrors that sparkled as the lights fell on them. A seating area with tables and chairs surrounded the dance floor. There was a raised section beside the bar with a few tables. There was another larger raised tier with tables and chairs on the right at the rear of the club that was very popular.

The club would hold three hundred fifty to four hundred and it was ready to go.

Mieler said, "I'll rent this to you for $350 a month, and you can use my beer license."

So, Bobby rented it from him and named it "The Embers Hilton Underground."

"And man, it was the biggest money-maker we ever had," Bobby said. "My brother, my mother, and my daddy ran it and we decided to let ladies in free Monday through Thursday. Man, the ladies flocked there. Within thirty days, you couldn't get a room there.

The Embers Hilton Underground was an exciting venture for the band, with dreams of making it more than just a music venue. In fact, it even had a kitchen, sparking a wild idea—what if The Embers ran their own restaurant? Bobby Tomlinson, always open to new possibilities, thought he'd better seek some expert advice.

He reached out to his good friend, the legendary restaurateur Thad Eure. After giving Thad a grand tour of the club, Bobby waited for his thoughts. Thad, taking it all in, turned to Bobby with a sly grin and said, "You know, I can't play drums." Bobby laughed and replied, "And I sure can't cook."

Without missing a beat, Thad responded, "Then that's your answer—I'll steer clear of the drums and maybe you should pump the brakes on the restaurant idea."

And just like that, The Embers stayed in their lane—on stage, where they belonged.

"The Embers played The Embers Hilton Underground frequently and we had other great entertainers. Cortez Greer, sadly, was playing in that club the week he died.

"We also had The Showmen, Bill Pinkney's Original Drifters, The Vogues, Mickey and Sylvia, Cornelius

Brothers and Sister Rose, Sonny Turner' Platters, The Catalinas, Maurice Williams and the Zodiacs, and The Tams. There were lots of others too numerous to mention."

Paul Craver, trumpet player and band leader remembers an offer from Bobby Tomlinson and Bill Griffin from The Castaways Club. "They approached me and said, 'We've got so many gigs, we cannot handle them all. We've got the Hilton Underground in Raleigh, the Hilton in Greensboro, and the Hilton in Winston-Salem. We want to put together a band to take care of the overflow of The Embers. And what we really want to do is bring back the name The O'Kaysions of "I'm A Girl Watcher" fame.' So, I did. We patterned the band after The Embers and had the time of our life handling the overflow of The Embers dates. We did all the Hiltons, the Holiday Inns, The Landmark Resort Hotel, and more. We were kind of a carbon copy of The Embers."

Following the Center Court Lounge LP, The Embers picked up a song they heard Cortez Greer perform at their Hilton Underground Embers Club, "I'm Gonna Do Beautiful Things For You."

B.J. Thomas had first recorded "Beautiful Things" in 1975 but it was Cortez Greer's cover that was being played on Carolina radio stations. Cortez recorded the song in 1976 and died November 4th of that same year while in Raleigh performing at the Embers Hilton Underground. He died of carbon monoxide poisoning due to a gas leak in the cabin in which he was staying.

The Embers recorded the song at Mega Sound Studio in Bailey, North Carolina. Their treatment was different and Jackie Gore's strong vocals made it one of their most popular songs. The flip side is also notable. It was a cover of Joe Cocker's "You Are So Beautiful" by new Ember Craig Woolard who would prove he could deliver big songs in addition to Gore.

The Embers' "Beautiful Things" was ranked No. 3 for the year 1976 in John Hook's retroactive year-end chart published in his 2006 Beach Music Encyclopedia.

As word spread, the crowds grew. You never knew who would be there. Stories abounded about big-name rockers in town for concerts at the colleges and nearby Reynold's Coliseum who found their way to The Embers Hilton Underground after their performances. KISS came into the club. Elton John's band dropped by, and Nigel Olsson, Elton's long-time drummer, is said to have fallen in love with a local girl he met there that night, whom he later married.

The Embers Hilton Underground became a favorite hangout for the pro wrestlers who filmed at WRAL TV. Many of the wrestlers stayed at the hotel. Pro wrestling was huge at the time. They became "regulars" and would congregate in the area that became known as "the far back upper level." Some of the wrestlers who enjoyed themselves there were Rick Flair, Andre the Giant, Dusty Rhodes, Wahoo McDaniels, Ricky Steamboat, Gene and Ole Anderson, Blackjack Mulligan, and Paul Jones.

Somehow, the wrestlers creatively adjusted the lighting in the area so they would not be the center of attention. They should not be seen in public together as they were "mortal enemies." The wrestlers were also known to invite the band and some of the audience to their rooms to continue to party after closing time.

One night, after closing, a door had been locked that led to the rooms. Bobby heard glass breaking and walked up where he could see, and found Wahoo McDaniels standing there. He said to Bobby, "Send me a bill, I didn't want to walk around."

The club also became renowned for dancing. With great music, the instructors and students who were involved at Arthur Murray Dance Studio nearby would come by after the dance studio closed at 10 p.m.

"The Embers Hilton Underground was a great place for rehearsals," Bobby recalled. "With the new lineup, we were there frequently and started practicing some new songs in late 1977 and 1978 and Jackie had written an original song. It was a busy time."

"We were there for several years, but when state law changed and liquor-by-the-drink became legal, the hotel decided to take the club back over. However, they asked Bobby if they would still play for the club, and Bobby said, "I don't think so."

With a twinkle in his eye, he added, "They lasted about six months."

Chapter 21

THE 1970s MARKED a significant period of growth, adaptation, and revival for The Embers and the beach music scene. Bobby's decision to stay true to their roots while incorporating new influences allowed them to navigate the changing musical landscape successfully. The partnerships they formed, the innovative performances they delivered, and the memorable moments they created all contributed to their enduring legacy.

Through their relentless touring, engaging performances, and strategic releases, The Embers played a central role in keeping the spirit of beach music alive. Their influence extended far beyond the coastal regions, reaching inland cities and inspiring a new generation of fans. The revival of beach music in the later 1970s was a celebration of a cultural heritage that continues to bring joy and unity to people of all ages.

As Bobby looks back on this vibrant period in music history, it's clear that The Embers were more than just a band, they were ambassadors of a genre that embodied the essence of summer, community, and the simple pleasure of dancing the night away. Their legacy lives on, reminding us of the timeless appeal of beach music and the power of a great song to bring people together.

In the late 1970s, as disco fever began to wane and the music scene splintered into punk, new wave, and a host of other genres, a nostalgic movement was quietly brewing along the Southeast coast of the United States.

It was a revival of beach music—a soulful, rhythmic sound that had once been the soundtrack to endless summer nights on the shores of the Carolinas. At the forefront of this revival was a band that had been synonymous with the genre since its inception—The Embers.

The Embers, formed in Raleigh, North Carolina in the late 1950s, were already legends in the beach music scene by the time the 1980s rolled around. Their sound was a seamless blend of R&B, soul, and rock and roll, perfectly crafted to get people dancing. But as musical tastes shifted in the 1970s, even The Embers faced the challenge of staying relevant. This challenge, however, was met with a strategic move that would not only cement their legacy but also reignite the passion for beach music across the Southeast.

In the mid to late 1970s, things began to pick up on the beach music scene. The crowds seemed to get bigger. College students and younger fans, eager for good music and a fun time, started showing up in droves. Their enthusiasm was noticeable and contagious.

Gerald Davis recalled, "One day in 1978 we were booked for an event at Lake Wheeler, near Raleigh, that I think may have been the very first beach music festival ever. It was The Embers, Cornelius Brothers and Sister Rose, The Showmen, The Drifters, and The Tams. Twenty thousand people showed up at that concert. It was an all-day event. It started at eleven o'clock in the morning and ended at seven o'clock that night and we were on about three or four in the afternoon and we left straight from there and went to the Hilton Underground Embers Club and played that night. Talk about being exhausted.

"But people saw what money could be made off of a beach music festival. And from that point on, they popped up everywhere. There was one in Greensboro and there was that big Emerald Isle Beach Music Festival and those people took it and ran with it and theirs got huge."

Returning home from a gig in the late 1970s, Jackie Gore couldn't stop thinking about these changes. He sat down in his kitchen, guitar in hand, and began to strum. "The lady I was married to at the time said we had a lot of younger people following our band around in the 60s and the 70s," Jackie recalled. "LaRue said, 'Jackie, why don't you write a song for all of these young people? Just write a song about beach music because you've got such a young following of people and kind of let it just be their song.'"

Inspired by his wife's words, Jackie let his fingers glide over the strings. "I was sitting in my kitchen with my guitar," he explained, "and I just came up with the tune which popped into my head. 'I love beach music, I always have and I always will.'"

The melody flowed naturally and Jackie started incorporating titles from old beach music songs. "I took titles like '60-Minute Man,' 'Walking Up a One-Way Street,' and 'Ooo, Ms. Grace,' and just wove them into the format. That's how the song came about."

Before long, Jackie's three-minute-and-five-second song included the titles of nine beach music standards and even a salute to a fellow Carolina band. He added fan favorites "Up On The Roof," "Under The Boardwalk," "Summertime's Calling Me," "39-21-46," "What Kind of Fool," and "It Will Stand."

"He brought it to rehearsal one day," Gerald Davis recalled. "He said, 'The name of the song is, 'I Love Beach Music.' I thought, that's kind of strange, titling a song after a genre of music, but little did I know what was to come. We sat down and worked it out."

The band began rehearsing the song at The Embers Hilton Underground, where it was likely first played for a live audience. The reaction was overwhelmingly positive. The crowd's excitement and the band's energy created an unforgettable atmosphere. They knew they had something special.

JD Cash, recording star and entertainer, reported, "I hadn't been home in two or three years and when I got home, I looked in the paper and saw The Embers were playing at the Hilton Underground in Raleigh. Well, I had to go. I wanted to see my old friend Durwood and everybody.

"That particular night I walked in and there was no Durwood and no Big John. They had just played their last job, maybe the night before. And it was actually the first night, I think, that Craig Woolard and Gerald Davis had joined the band. And it's the first time I heard Jackie Gore sing "I Love Beach Music." They hadn't even recorded it yet. That started the second wave of the Embers. I mean, they never lost any popularity. Craig was a great addition to the band. Everybody thought they'd fall apart. Well, they didn't.

"And then around 1980, they added Johnny Barker. And that's when it exploded. I mean, he was the missing link, because he's such a powerful musician—just the best writer, arranger, producer. He, Bobby, and Gerald became the backbone with Craig, Jackie, and Johnny Hopkins up front. It just couldn't miss. The group had an aura around it that'll never exist again. I mean, there was a magic. When they would play at the Landmark, they'd have to put them in the ballroom. The club wasn't big enough. I'm literally serious. I worked down there. And it was packed every night."

Soon after, The Embers headed to Mega Studio in Bailey, NC to record the song "I Love Beach Music." They took that master to Reflection Studio in Charlotte to add finishing touches before releasing it as eEe 1001. The flip side featured another Jackie Gore original, "Why Did You Leave Me."

Jackie remembered, "'I Love Beach Music' was an instant hit. When we recorded it, I sent a copy to a lot of radio DJs in the area. Chris Beachley, who owns The Wax Museum in Charlotte, a famous old record store where he sold beach music songs, called me and said, 'Jackie, I

Arranged and Produced by The Embers Recorded At Reflection Sound Studios Charlotte, N.C.

EEE 1001
STEREO
Time 3:05
EEE Ltd. Pub
BMI

I LOVE BEACH MUSIC
(Music and Lyrics by Jackie Gore)
THE EMBERS

I LOVE BEACH MUSIC
THE EMBERS
EEE 1001

"I love beach music..., I always have and I always will, There ain't no other kind of music in the world that gives me quite the thrill."

No superlatives can describe just how great this record is!!! The lyrics and beat together typify the total spectrum of beach music.

Jackie Gore and crew run through references to "Up On The Roof", "Under the Boardwalk", "Summertime's Calling Me" only to stop briefly to chime their voices as they do in "Far Away Places", then back to "Ooh-Ooh-Ooh Ms. Grace, 39-21-40 Shape, What Kind of Fool Do You Think I Am, and forever and ever, It Will Stand!" (By God, that's us!)

"That old beer drinkin' music, shaggin' kind of music, like you hear at O.D."

PREDICTION: This record will challenge Ms. Grace for the hottest beach record this summer! If you never buy another beach record, buy this one!

cannot believe this song that you have written. This is the greatest thing that's ever been done for beach music.' He was instrumental in promoting 'I Love Beach Music,' which has become the national anthem of beach music, or so they say."

The song quickly gained traction on Southern radio stations, becoming a major hit in the Carolinas and receiving airplay throughout the Southeast. It was huge in Atlanta and helped fuel the revival of interest in beach music in the 1980s. As stations in the South added "I Love Beach Music" to their playlists, it introduced many listeners to the genre's classics for the first time.

Julian Fowler, a well-known beach music historian and collector explains, "From 1958 to 1979, The Embers was a solid performing group, but once 'I Love Beach Music' came into play, everything changed. Suddenly, everybody wanted The Embers to perform. It became the song for which they were known and for a while, nobody else would play it. But today it has become a standard for beach music fans and many bands now play it."

The initial run of vinyl records sold out rapidly. The Embers returned to Reflection Studio in late 1979 to produce a new version of the song with added strings, guided by producer Johnny Barker, the keyboard player for The Catalinas, known for his production and arrangement skills. This version, released as EEE 1002, was followed by a stereo version released as EEE 1004 in 1980, which was featured on The Embers' "I Love Beach Music" LP.

Later that year Johnny Barker played for a New Year's Eve party at the Statesville Country Club as a member of The Catalinas. The very next night, January 1, 1980, Johnny started a week-long engagement at The

Boondocks in Greensboro as a full-time member of The Embers. He would have a major impact on The Embers' "Golden Years" during the 1980s.

Donny Trexler, of Donny and Susan Trexler, remarked, "Because musicians acquire a fan base, when there's a change, you're going to have a lot of people unhappy. But with every change The Embers made, they acquired more new fans, and it just kept getting better and better each time. The show must go on, and they kept the show going on."

CHAPTER 22

THE "I LOVE BEACH MUSIC" LP itself was an instant success. Containing eleven songs and the new version of "I Love Beach Music," "Cheaters Never Win," "I'm Gonna Do Beautiful Things For You," and "You Are So Beautiful" all got airplay in the beach music market. The album was highly advertised by record stores from Virginia to Florida. It, like the 45, was a big record for The Embers.

Also, that year The Embers released a single version of "Cheaters Never Win" from the LP. On the flip side, they placed another medley of strung-together classic R&B songs performed to a shag beat. The idea for the medley came from Marion Carter of Ripete Records who had noted the recent success of the "Stars on 45" records that had emerged from the disco-clubs and The Embers' "I Love Beach Music." The Embers' Gerald Davis worked his magic by combining a dozen Carolina beach classics. Songs included were: "Having A Party," "Across The Street," "Ain't No Big Thing," "He Will Break Your Heart," "Fool In Love," "Rocking Pneumonia," "How Sweet It Is," "Little Darling I Need You," "Ms. Grace," "39-21-46," "Hey Baby," and "I Love Beach Music."

In 1981, Chris Beachley tabulated the very first All Time Beach Music Top 50 chart for his "It Will Stand" magazine. "I Love Beach Music" came in at #25.

Atlanta radio station WQXI had a two-hour beach music show on Sunday afternoons during the summer of 1982. Air personality Kelly McCoy and Atlanta beach music historian Buddy Hawkins compiled their version of Atlanta's All-Time Top 10 Beach Music songs and rated the song #5.

Beach Music historian John Hook retroactively re-created beach music charts for the years 1946-2006 for a book he released in 2007. He placed "I Love Beach Music" as the #1 song of the year for 1979 on John Hook's Beach Music Top 40 charts.

John said this about the first time he heard The Embers. "I was at The Treehouse in Charlotte standing at the bar talking to two different ladies while trying to decide which might be a good nominee for a late date when all of a sudden, I heard this unique sound coming from the stage, 'Bum, bum, bum, bum, bum, bum wee-ooo.' I turned around and asked 'Who's the band?' They said, 'The Embers.' And I said, 'Wow!'"

In the 2014 documentary film by Skip Crayton and Bill Benners "*The Embers - The Heart and Soul of Beach Music,*" John Hook remarked, "When 'I Love Beach Music' came out, that was the beginning of that whole new golden era of Beach Music. The first golden era was the

60s. The 80s, led by the Embers' 'I Love Beach Music' exploded it all wide open."

Skip Crayton, co-author and one of the producers for McBryde Films' 2014 documentary remarked during an interview with Jackie Gore, "Well, 'I Love Beach Music' certainly has the most identifiable first five notes of any song, maybe after Beethoven's Fifth."

In 2023, Surf 94.9 FM in Myrtle Beach, SC, released its All-Time Beach Music Top 40 Chart to include songs from 1980 to 2022, ranking "I Love Beach Music" at #3. The song was also placed in the Carolina Beach Music Hall of Fame at the 2023 Carolina Beach Music Awards ceremony.

Jackie's inspiration had turned into a timeless classic. The Embers' "I Love Beach Music" became more than a song, it was an anthem that captured the spirit of an entire genre and era. The song's journey from a casual suggestion in a kitchen to a staple of beach music history is a testament to the power of music to unite and inspire generations.

Reflecting on those early days, Jackie Gore smiled. "The reaction was beyond anything we could have imagined," he said. "We were just doing what we loved, but to see so many people embrace the song and make it their own was incredible."

As The Embers continued to tour and perform, "I Love Beach Music" was always a highlight of their set. Fans old and new would sing along, their voices mingling with the crashing waves and the warm Carolina breeze. The song, much like the beach music it celebrated, was timeless, rooted in nostalgia yet forever fresh, a melody that evoked the carefree days of summer and the joy of dancing barefoot on the sand.

Carolina Beach Music wasn't just music, it was a movement, a community, and a way of life. And at the heart of that movement was The Embers, whose dedication to their craft and their fans helped keep the spirit of beach music alive. From local gigs to national stages, from small-town radio stations to major airwaves, "I Love Beach Music" was the song that brought people together, transcending age and background, and celebrating the simple, enduring pleasure of good music and good times.

Then something magical happened.

Chapter 23

IN APRIL OF 1980, The Embers were on stage at The Emerald Isle Beach Music Festival at the Holiday Inn Travel Park overlooking a wide beach on the Atlantic Ocean. There were about twenty thousand fans there that day to see Bill Pinkney's Drifters, Chairmen of the Board, Cornelius Brothers and Sister Rose, The Castaways, and The Embers.

While the Embers were on stage performing what had become their signature song, the crowd's energy surged. Halfway through the performance, someone handed Jackie a Budweiser. He held it high, grinning from ear to ear and continued singing the song. But when he came to the part of the song that contained its title, he inserted "I Love Bud-weiser!" and  the crowd went wild. Jackie's unscripted change in lyrics caught on. The crowd responded by singing along and waving cans of Budweiser high in the air.

"Eight or ten thousand people holding their Budweiser cans up, singing 'I Love Budweiser.' It was a natural for Budweiser," Jackie said.

After the concert, Tomlinson spoke to some of the

Anheuser-Busch people backstage and they were still in awe. They said, "That was incredible." As everyone went home that night, no one fully realized what was about to happen.

A few weeks later, The Embers were back at the Landmark Resort Hotel for a two-week stint around Mother's Day. The Budweiser distributor in Myrtle Beach, Spud Spadoni of Better Brands, was an ardent fan of the band. Bobby explained, "His son was an Embers freak. He loved us. And he talked with his dad about The Embers doing a Budweiser commercial and his dad said, 'Do the commercial, and I'll send it.'"

So, The Embers recorded a sample commercial at a Raleigh studio, incorporating the lyrics, "I Love

Budweiser, ain't no other beer in the whole wide world. It gives me such a thrill."

Bobby said, "We sent the recording to Spud in Myrtle Beach and the local guys got it hooked up with the national people and they wrote us back and told us we were too local. We accepted that, but we kept doing the commercial everywhere we played."

Throughout the Southeast from Virginia Beach to New Orleans, they performed their Budweiser tribute, winning over Budweiser distributors who clamored for copies of the commercial.

All of a sudden, the Anheuser-Busch headquarters in St. Louis was bombarded by distributors requesting a commercial they didn't have. Two weeks later, Bobby got a call—August Busch, head of the brewery, has given his approval to explore the concept and they'll be in touch.

"Then I got a call from Bob Fuller out of Cary, the Budweiser rep for the Carolinas and Virginia and we set up a meeting at the pizza parlor my parents ran. I took all of our albums, t-shirts, hats—everything I could find and I met with him."

Bobby chuckled at the memory of the meeting saying "He sat down, looked at me, and said, 'What exactly do you want from Budweiser?' A lot of times I say things that are kind of crazy and I said, 'We don't want any more than you give Lou Rawls.'" Bobby sat back and laughed aloud thinking back on the moment.

Fuller took the request back to St. Louis and the next call was from their advertising agency. They asked, "When can you do this commercial?" Bobby replied, "When can *you* do it?"

A couple of weeks later, they're in the Arthur Smith Studio again recording a Budweiser commercial. Fuller said, "We can't do what you did because you can't promote the effects of beer—'It gives me such a thrill.'"

So, the lyrics were changed to "Budweiser, king of beers."

They crafted two versions—their signature "I Love Budweiser" and one with Budweiser's current slogan, "This Bud's for You." The session was long but productive, and the band forged a strong rapport with the Budweiser team.

After the recording session, Bobby drove the ad executive back to the airport and said, "What happens now?"

"I take this back to August and if he doesn't like it, it's over. But if he likes it, you're in." The ad executive then added, "This stuff's good. *Really* good. I thought I was going to be dealing with a bunch of rednecks."

Bobby smirked, "You were."

Chapter 24

A FEW WEEKS PASSED, and Bobby received a call with the verdict—August Busch, head of the brewery, loved the commercials.

Soon, anywhere you were, you could turn the radio on and you'd hear these commercials. Gerald Davis said, "We thought it was going to be a local spot. But when the royalty checks started coming in, they were from everywhere. New York, Chicago, and L.A." The ad was airing not just in the Carolinas, and the big cities, it was airing all across the country. A friend of Bobby's in Los Angeles said he even heard it at a Dodger baseball game, marveling at how The Embers had hit the big time.

"So, a few months later, I go to my mailbox," Bobby said, "and I pick up this envelope about three-quarters of an inch thick. And it's from 'Talent Residuals,' which I know nothing about. So, I open this envelope and it's full of checks. And I go up to the adding machine and start adding them up, and it's $24,000 in this envelope. So, I called St. Louis and I said, 'Do y'all ever make mistakes?' And the woman with whom I was speaking laughed and said, 'What are you talking about?' I said, 'Well, I just got an envelope from Talent Residuals and there's $24,000 in this envelope.' She said, 'Oh, that's right. This thing is doing great, they're playing everywhere. You can probably expect another one in three months.'

That was the first of many residual payments that would total nearly $300,000 over the next three years and the partnership with Budweiser lasted more than a decade. It was a lucrative and iconic chapter in The Embers' storied career.

Jackie added, "As a result, we started playing all of their conventions

all over the country. Boca Raton, Florida, San Diego, Chicago. They took us to Hawaii twice."

Gerald Davis added, "They flew our whole families out

to Hawaii for a four-day trip. We only had to play for two hours. And then we had three or four days to do anything we wanted to in Hawaii."

"Johnny Hopkins added, "We did lots and lots of Budweiser things through the years. They would fly us to all of these different places all over the country. That was a wonderful relationship. They are great people to work with."

Jackie nodded, "As a result of my song 'I Love Beach Music,' our band was playing all over the country for Budweiser."

The Budweiser years remained a shining example of The Embers' ingenuity and enduring appeal. This playful moment, where Jackie commemorated a fan's offer of a beer into song, became an iconic moment in beach music history and commercial success.

The success of "I Love Beach Music" led to the release of an album of the same name. The album was a collection of classic beach music tunes and original compositions, all imbued with The Embers' signature style. It served as a comprehensive introduction to the genre for newcomers and a nostalgic trip for longtime fans. The album's popularity helped to solidify The Embers' role as the torchbearers of beach music, breathing new life into the genre and bringing it back into the spotlight.

Riding on the wave of success, The Embers continued to innovate and expand their influence. In 1981, they released "Embers Beach Medley," a masterful mix of beach music classics that showcased their versatility and deep understanding of the genre. The medley became a staple at their live shows, further endearing them to their audience and solidifying their reputation as the ultimate beach music band.

After a short period without a club, Bobby was soon back in the club business with a new Embers Club located in King's Plaza shopping center on Capital Boulevard in Raleigh. The Grand Opening was held in November 1979 with The Embers as headliners. It was gone by June 1980.

"We just never could quite make it go like we wanted to," said Tomlinson. "It had been several clubs previously and no one was able to make it click. We just couldn't get the crowd we needed on a regular basis to make a go of it."

But it was not a total bust, as something good emerged from it. In fact, it was very good, and it happened one winter night when The Embers were playing at the King's Plaza Embers Club. A new management group had taken over the Landmark Resort Hotel, the high-rise hotel on the South end of Myrtle Beach where The Embers had played regularly in the mid-70s.

"In early 1980, Don Ross, the new manager came to see our show in Raleigh one night," remembers Tomlinson. "He came up and introduced himself after one of our sets. And he said 'I was told that if I was going to make The Landmark successful again, most people told me I should put beach music in the club.' At that time, most of the beach music was up in North Myrtle Beach.

So, he said 'I was told I needed to put The Embers back in here,' so we talked and we came to an agreement.

"Ross wanted The Embers for a ten-week engagement during the summer. He requested we play Easter, Memorial Day, July 4th, and Labor Day weeks and fill out a ten-week schedule of The Embers' choosing. The deal was on."

When the summer season began the band was given rooms. The first week they were there, there was a bowl of fruit in everybody's room with a note from Ross saying "Looking forward to a great summer." And it was that way every year the whole time they played."

It was a typical hotel club. You came up the elevator from the lobby and you came into a larger lobby. The Coquina Ballroom was to your right and the Coquina Club was to your left. The club held about three hundred people and had a bar on your left when you walked in. The stage was directly across from the bar at a narrow end of the club.

"There were windows on both sides and our back was to the wall and it had a stairwell behind us which we used to go out when Jackie would do Raymond Massey for thirty minutes. It was a great club.

"We played there on Monday, Tuesday, Wednesday, and Thursday nights. We were drawing so many people that on Friday and Saturday, he would move us to either the downstairs ballroom that held six hundred plus or to the upstairs ballroom that held about a thousand, depending on whichever one was available. "When we were playing, there was always a big crowd," Bobby said. "It was wall to wall. They were making a killing on us.

"At that time, we were wearing those clothes from Florida and we were doing our floor shows. Our opening for the floor shows was the Rocky Movie theme, "Eye of The Tiger." It was dramatic. We had graduated to a great floor show that included a light show with tiers of lights in the back and a smoke machine. We gave them a show."

"I think it was just a situation where the timing of entertainment like that coming to the area, and the people who had grown up with what The Embers had always done were now getting a little older and ready to sit down and watch something like that."

Chapter 25

During the 70s and 80s, music was shifting again. FM radio stations were taking over the airwaves. Album-oriented rock stations were playing the likes of Led Zeppelin, Pink Floyd, and The Rolling Stones.

Disco was fading, but stars like Donna Summer and The Bee Gees still held on. In the world of pop and R&B, Michael Jackson, Diana Ross, and Stevie Wonder were dominating airplay. But in the Southeast, another movement was gaining momentum—one fueled by a sentimental longing for the past.

At the heart of this resurgence was The Embers, a band already synonymous with beach music. Their 1979 release, "I Love Beach Music," became an anthem for a genre many thought was fading into memory. The song reignited a passion for the soulful rhythms and breezy harmonies that had once filled the dance floors of the Carolinas in the 1950s and 1960s. As the 1980s unfolded, The Embers would lead the charge, not just with their recordings but with a relentless touring schedule that drew old and new fans alike back to the joyful sounds of beach music.

Myrtle Beach, South Carolina, long known as the heart of beach music and a pioneer of the shag dance, became a central hub for this revival. Clubs like The Spanish Galleon and Fat Harold's Beach Club hosted regular Embers' performances, drawing enormous crowds eager to dance to the infectious beat of "I Love Beach Music." The band's live shows were electric, blending tight musicianship with choreographed dance moves, engaging showmanship, and a dynamic energy that turned every performance into a celebration.

"Myrtle Beach was like our second home," recalled drummer Bobby Tomlinson. "We played there so often that people would plan their vacations around our shows. When we hit the stage, the place would be packed. The energy was electric, and every night felt like a party."

But the revival wasn't confined to the coast. Inland cities like Atlanta began to embrace beach music with a fervor that mirrored the coastal scene. Between 1980 and 1983, Atlanta saw the rise of over fifteen beach music clubs, including iconic venues like Buckhead Beach and Ocean Drive South, bringing the spirit of Myrtle Beach to the heart of the city. Festivals like the Atlanta Beach Music Festival and the Jekyll Island Beach Music Festival drew large crowds, further spreading the genre's infectious rhythms and carefree spirit.

The formation of the Association of Carolina Shag Clubs (ACSC) in the early 1980s also played a pivotal role in the genre's inland expansion. Shag dancers flocked to events and competitions, drawn together by their shared love of the music and the dance that embodied its essence. It wasn't long before these shag events became a central fixture in cities far from the coastal Carolina hotspots.

"The revival of beach music wasn't just about nostalgia," Bobby explained. "It was about community. The music brought people together, and the dance gave them a way to express themselves."

The success of "I Love Beach Music" catapulted The Embers to new heights in the 1980s. Their performances became legendary, and the band's lineup, featuring Bobby Tomlinson, Jackie Gore, Craig Woolard, Gerald Davis, Johnny Hopkins, and Johnny Barker, became known for their camaraderie and seamless musicianship.

"We had a group of guys who not only played well together but genuinely liked each other. That kind of connection showed in our performances," Bobby recalled.

With their strong lineup and growing popularity, The Embers hit the road, playing at clubs, festivals, and events throughout the Southeast. One of their most significant stops was the Landmark Resort Hotel in Myrtle Beach, where they held ten-week summer contracts, playing to packed houses every night. "We got so popular down there that you couldn't get a room at the hotel when we played," Bobby shared. "People made their vacation plans around us."

In 1980, The Embers recorded a live album at the Landmark Resort titled "The Embers: A Landmark Performance." The double LP captured the energy of their live shows, offering fans a seventy-five-minute recording that showcased the best of their performances. "Capturing that live energy was important to us," Bobby explained. "Our shows were special, and we wanted to preserve that magic on record."

As the 1980s progressed, beach music experienced a full-fledged renaissance. Bands like The Catalinas, Chairmen of the Board, The Tams, and Band of Oz joined the revival, releasing new material that blended the nostalgic rhythms of beach music with contemporary influences. This new wave of music, led by The Embers, helped keep the genre fresh and relevant in a rapidly changing musical landscape.

"We never wanted to abandon our roots," Bobby emphasized. "But we also wanted to keep things exciting, to make sure the music evolved while staying true to what made it great in the first place."

For The Embers, the 1980s marked a golden era. Their relentless touring schedule, dynamic performances, and strategic releases, such as "Embers Beach Medley," solidified their place as beach music icons. Through their music, they not only kept the spirit of beach music alive but inspired a new generation of fans and musicians.

But the band's success wasn't just limited to their live performances. "The success of 'I Love Beach Music' was incredible," Bobby recalls. "It opened so many doors for us." And one of them was at Budweiser World Headquarters where The Embers began that wonderful decade of singing nationally-circulated radio and television commercials for Anheuser-Busch.

As Bobby Tomlinson reflected on this era, he summed it up best saying, "We weren't just a band. We were ambassadors for a sound, for a feeling. Beach music is more than just music—it's about bringing people together, about capturing that joy and that sense of community. And that's what we lived for."

The Embers' contributions during this time weren't just pivotal, they were foundational to the resurgence of beach music, ensuring that its infectious rhythms and timeless melodies would continue to bring joy to audiences for decades to come.

Gerald Davis told of another time when bringing joy to their audiences backfired. "We had gotten to this job in a little town in South Carolina in the early 80s and the dressing room was right behind the stage. There happened to be a bunch of used old ladies' clothes—everything from granny's clothes on down—hanging on a rack in our dressing room.

"We must have had a lot of time on our hands because we were sitting there thinking how funny it would be if we all dressed in those old ladies' clothes and came out on stage because we were doing four shows. So, we did it. The whole band dressed in those women's clothes and we were walking around getting the biggest kick out of each other and looking at how funny we looked.

So, when it was time to play, we walked out there in those used old ladies' clothes, picked up our instruments, and looked at the audience. The crowd sat there stunned. It totally *bombed*, but we were stuck. We had to do the whole first set that way," he laughed.

Chapter 26

THE SPRING OF 1981 found the Embers on a roll. They had followed up their 1979 smash "I Love Beach Music" with a new album and had a new hit on the beach music radio stations, a twelve-song medley titled "Embers Beach Music Medley 81." They were also on the radio nationwide singing "I Love Budweiser" in commercials for the Anheuser-Busch branding campaign. And they were in the second year of a multi-year, summer-long contract at The Landmark Hotel Resort Hotel in the center of Myrtle Beach.

The "Embers Beach Music Medley 81" captured the essence of beach music," Bobby explains. "It was a trip down memory lane for our fans and a reminder of why they loved the genre."

Doug McKendrick, a UNC graduate who wanted to replicate the clubs he frequented during his college years in Chapel Hill, had purchased the Atlanta club known as Animal Crackers. It was a unique club at the corner of Peachtree and Pharr Road in an area that was known as Buckhead. Animal Crackers was a storied club with a working Ferris Wheel inside.

With the closing of the club on June 8 of '81, McKendrick took possession, redecorated it as a boardwalk, hauled in sand, and reopened to the public on Friday, June 12, as "Buckhead Beach."

Before the grand opening, McKendrick sent out 500 invitations to attend a private opening on Thursday night.

The invitation was a custom 45 rpm record hand-delivered earlier in the week. The A-side was a new song by The Embers titled "At the Buckhead Beach." The flip side was titled "A Special Invitation to a Private Party at the Buckhead Beach."

McKendrick had hired local songwriter Tim McCabe to pen the song. Smith-McNeal Advertising Agency's Shay McNeal and Terri Evans are also credited on the record.

A few days before the private opening, McKendrick flew The Embers to Atlanta on a Sunday via charter from Myrtle Beach where they were booked for the summer. Bobby Tomlinson recalls it was an all-day recording session leaving Myrtle Beach airport at 9 a.m. and returning from Atlanta by 5 p.m. for their contracted performance at 8:30 p.m.

"We were given the lyrics to the song when we boarded and practiced them during the flight," said Tomlinson. In Atlanta, they were shuttled to Bill Lowery's famed Master Sound Studio where they spent half a day recording "At the Buckhead Beach."

"Recording 'Buckhead Beach' was special," Bobby says. "It was a tribute to what would become a legendary nightclub and the incredible fans there."

McKendrick, a huge Embers fan, hand-delivered five hundred copies of the record in a stylish jacket cover with the club logo. Although extremely hard to find, the record did receive significant airplay in the South.

Robert Ray, an Atlanta falsetto-voiced singer happened by Master Sound Studio that afternoon and sang along on a playback of the new song. The producers liked what they heard, pulled him into the studio, and laid down the additional track.

From McCabe's lyrics:
BUCKHEAD BEACH CHORUS
I remember when we did the shag,
And Papa had himself a brand-new bag,
A Carolina boy and a Georgia Peach,
At the Buckhead Beach...

The flip side is the invite to the party. It begins with the Embers' chorus of Buckhead Beach. A deejay's voice track spills the invite details:

> "Memories are alive again and it's fun and summertime every day. Thursday, June 11 is your day in the sun at the Buckhead Beach. Join us for our private opening from 8 to 10 p.m. at the Buckhead Beach, Peachtree and Pharr Road. It's gonna be a flashback."

Then the song wraps around to close out the sixty-second invitation.

The 45 was released by Buckhead Beach as the invite to the VIP event on the Star Song record label. The number of 45s pressed is unknown but may have been as few as five hundred. It did not chart on the year-end Beach Music Chart but received significant airplay in the Southeast.

It was a huge hit in Atlanta and ruled the airways in 1981. "At the Buckhead Beach" was included on the Embers' 25th Anniversary album released in 1983.

The club sprang to life with the private opening on Thursday, June 11, 1981. Over the next almost three years, more than sixty bands performed. It became the hangout for college students and was the subject of numerous articles in the Atlanta newspapers, Billboard magazine, and a two-page spread in the Georgia Tech yearbook.

The record is hard to find and is among the rarest of the Carolina beach music releases. It has sold for as much as $1200 in published auctions.

Chapter 27

1982 WAS A LANDMARK YEAR for The Embers, marked by the release of "This One's For You," an album featuring a thirty-eight-song, sixteen-plus-minute beach music medley. It would also see a "live" album recorded at the Myrtle Beach Hotel that became Beach Music Central. This ambitious project, "This One's For You," showcased the band's dedication to preserving and celebrating beach music.

Encouraged by the success of the Embers' Beach Music Medley '81, Gerald, working closely with Craig Woolard, expanded the twelve-song medley into an unbelievable thirty-eight-song, sixteen-minute version. Titled "Embers Beach Medley," the song took up one entire side of The Embers' 1982 LP. The additional twenty-six songs that were added read like the all-time favorites of Beach Music. It most likely remains the longest-recorded medley in beach music circles.

Other songs on the album included Craig's lead vocals on "Always In Love." Johnny Barker's work on arrangements was on full display with this LP, and he is credited with writing the song "Love Me." Jackie Gore is in command of his terrific cover of the melodic standard "Canadian Sunset" and wrote the lyrics and sang lead on "Take Care of You For Me."

On November 21, the First Annual Beach Music Awards Show was held at the Myrtle Beach Convention Center. This star-studded event featured the cream of the crop of the Carolina Beach Music genre and numerous celebrity entertainers who were on hand to present and make quick appearance spots during the show.

The night before the inaugural Beach Music Awards, Myrtle Beach was alive with anticipation. The Landmark Resort Hotel lounge, buzzing with beach music enthusiasts, was the place many had gathered to unwind before the big event, including some members of The Embers. What no one expected was the electrifying arrival of Mr. James Brown himself.

Beach Music historian John Hook recounted the moment vividly in conversation with Buzz Bolick. "Those North Carolina beach music bands used to always say if you couldn't go onstage and do the entire James Brown 'Live at the Apollo' album, which is a legendary rhythm and blues album, then you weren't a true beach music band. So here comes James Brown. He was a presenter for the awards program the next night and he walked into the club at the Landmark where we had all gathered to hang out.

"There was a band playing—I don't remember the band's name—and James walked up to the stage and asked if he could sing a couple of his songs with them. And he named a few of his songs and the band looked around confused. Members of The Embers scattered around the room guessed what was going on and rushed to the stage."

Craig laughed, "You got to be kidding me. Does *anybody* know? Oh yeah, *we* know!" So, Gerald Davis, Johnny Hopkins, Johnny Barker, and I grabbed our equipment and James asked if we knew this song and that song and we said, 'Whatever.' Bobby wasn't with us, but Bobby Davis, the drummer onstage, knew some of James' music. So, that night we backed up James Brown. There's a picture of us floating around on the internet showing us playing with James Brown."

John Hook remarked, "And that was when I saw a band who could do 'Live at the Apollo' all the way through and anything else James could come up with."

The following night at the Beach Music Awards, The

Embers were the final band to perform. They delivered the sixteen-song Embers Beach Music Medley before bringing James Brown out to perform "I Got You (I Feel Good)" with them as his backing band. The finale was "I Love Beach Music," with all of the presenters coming on stage to sing.

During the awards show, The Embers were named Group of the Year, and their album "This One's For You" won Album of the Year. Jackie Gore was honored as Male Vocalist of the Year. "Receiving those awards was a huge honor," Bobby reflects. "It was validation for all the hard work we put in and the love we had for our music."

Craig later said, "Playing for James Brown was really cool. I also met Ray Charles that weekend. I pressed the elevator button at the Landmark and when it opened, there was Ray Charles. He was there with his manager. I stepped in and said, 'Mr. Charles!' And he said, 'How you doing? How you doing?' I said, 'I just want to tell you, if you just let me shake your hand, I believe any illness I might have in my body would just jump right on out.' He stuck his hand out and I grabbed it and he said, 'God bless you, son. I hope it do.'"

In 1983, The Embers celebrated their 25th anniversary with a special LP released by HMC featuring caricatures of the six band members inside. The album,

recorded at Arthur Smith Studio in Charlotte and produced by Nick Hice at HMC, included twenty songs, featured the 1981 Embers Beach Music Medley, and a new version of "Far Away Places."

The Embers also released "Cool Me Out," with Craig Woolard on lead vocals. "Craig's voice brought a new dynamic to our music," Bobby says. "He had a unique style that resonated with our fans."

The band continued to be recognized for their showmanship and hits, being named the #1 Show Band for their performances and medleys. The second annual Beach Music Awards once again honored The Embers as Group of the Year.

In 1984, Zaymin Records released The Embers' third "live" album, "Vacation Live at the Landmark." Extended play records were becoming a big deal and being spun by DJs playing at clubs coast-to-coast. Nashville singer/songwriter/producer Turley Richards and Joe Boylan, a well-known producer, sought The Embers to record two original songs Richards had developed. Nashville promotions executive Rob Barber was on board to manage the project.

The idea was a double album. One would be a normal album of ten songs, including Richards' new songs. The second album featured on one side a special dance mix of an extended version of "Give Him Up." The other side contained what became a popular version of "It Must Be Him," a regular-length version of "Give Him Up," and an eleven-minute recording titled "Embers Rap Session" which provided DJs an opportunity to do a pseudo-interview with The Embers on vinyl providing pre-recorded answers to questions.

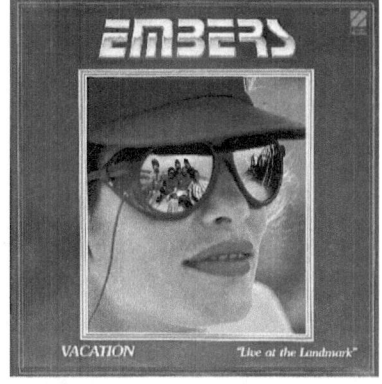

All were recorded live at The Landmark by Full Sail Productions' Remote Truck. Richardson wrote several original songs which appeared on the album. Rob Barber created the cover, an artistic treatment of a picture of his wife in sunglasses with The Embers reflected in the glasses.

Cliff Ellis, head basketball coach at Clemson University, heard The Embers perform at the Heritage Golf Tournament at Hilton Head in 1984. According to Cliff, the band's performance "knocked his socks off." This encounter sparked a friendship that would last for years.

In the 1986-87 basketball season, Clemson was undefeated when Cliff invited The Embers to sing the National Anthem at a home game against North Carolina State. The band delivered a stirring rendition, but to everyone's surprise, Clemson lost the game.

Cliff jokingly told the band afterward, "I thought it was great, but you'll never sing the National Anthem for me again!" Despite the loss, the friendship between Cliff and The Embers only grew stronger, leading to numerous collaborations over the years. When Cliff moved from Clemson to Auburn University to take on the head coaching role there, Cliff invited The Embers to perform at a party after an Auburn basketball game in the early 2000s.

Ellis recalled that the late Pat Dye, head football coach at Auburn from 1981-1991 was among those in attendance that night. Dye had been first introduced to The Embers and Beach Music when he coached at East Carolina University in Eastern North Carolina from 1974-1979. Ellis said, "Pat danced all night and told me he never had so much fun."

Bobby recalls with a laugh, "We played at plenty of Ellis' events, but we never again sang the National Anthem for him."

In 1985, Don Ross was let go by The Landmark Resort Hotel. Tomlinson recalls "I got a call that the new management wanted to talk to me. So, I walked in and sat down across the desk and this new manager and he said he just wanted to meet the band and go over some things. I said, 'Okay' and he started spouting off all these new rules. One of them was that he didn't want us to advertise for Budweiser anymore because they weren't getting anything out of it. I said "But you're getting the band and the band is a prestigious thing. He kept naming all these new changes and it was obvious we weren't going to agree.

"I informed him, 'You might not be aware of it but we haven't asked for a raise in three years. It is almost like a vacation to come down here, but now you're trying to make it a job. If you're going to make it a job, I'm going to have to charge you for a job. We'll play these two weeks, but from then on, the next time we come, we want a $1,500-a-week raise. He said he wouldn't pay that and that was our last two weeks at the Landmark."

Chapter 28

THE EMBERS BEGAN taking bookings at the Richmond, Virginia Marriott with Sam Zabowski and Steve Leonard. "Richmond welcomed us with open arms," Bobby recalls. "It was a new chapter and we embraced it with enthusiasm. We didn't miss a beat."

The band had met Sam Zabowski during the 70s in some of their South Carolina appearances. "When we again heard from him, he booked us at the Marriott Hotel in Richmond for several years and put us in the Marriott ballroom due to our drawing big crowds. There were always huge crowds.

"While he was there, Zabowski got involved in the community. He knew about beach music and he partnered with a prominent DJ there named Steve Leonard. And they started putting on these beach music concerts.

"Then he moved to Baltimore and called us again and we played for him at Oriole Stadium." He later moved to Florida and had The Embers play several events in the Marco Island area for a few years.

1986 saw the recording of "Christmas Memories," The Embers' first full Christmas album and possibly the first beach music Christmas LP. Recorded at Studio East in Charlotte, the album was produced by Nick Hice, Duke Hall, and Reece Culbreath, with executive producer Rob Barber and Barber Communication.

The album included tracks like "Blue Decorations" and "Santa Claus Is Coming To Town."

In 1987, Dunhill Compact Classics released the first Carolina Beach Music compilation CD under license from Ripete, including The Embers' "I Love Beach Music" on a twenty-five-song CD.

The band played at the Lawrenceville, VA, Live Beach Music Festival with Budweiser distributor Bobby Pecht, a festival that continued for several years. They also performed at the Virginia Port Festival and various Olympics-related events in Atlanta, Raleigh, and Charleston.

In the spring of 1987, North Myrtle Beach briefly became home to the sixth iteration of The Embers Club. Branded as Polo's Lounge & Embers Beach Club, this venture, nestled at 4530 Highway 17, was a short-lived chapter in the storied legacy of The Embers. Operating from April to July, it was a flash of excitement on the beach music scene, though its time was fleeting.

The club's inception came through a licensing agreement, a business decision and branding opportunity. "We granted the use of our Embers Beach Club brand for an agreed fee," Bobby Tomlinson recalled. The arrangement was brokered by the former owner of WNMB radio station, who saw an opportunity to capitalize on the iconic Embers name. Though the band wasn't directly involved in the day-to-day operations, they did grace the stage a few times, adding their unmistakable sound to the venue.

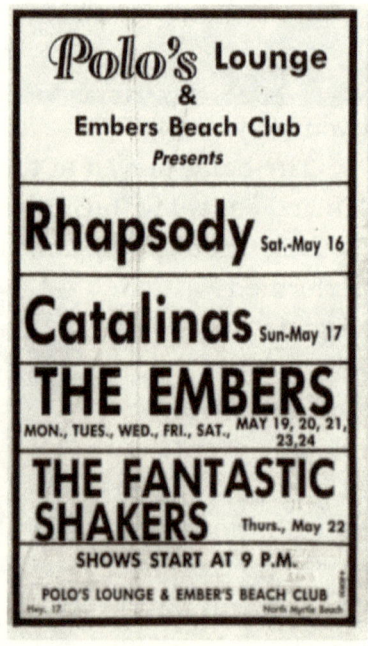

John Dockery was tasked with managing the club, and under his guidance, Polo's Lounge & Embers Beach Club opened with great fanfare. From April 16-19, The Embers formally inaugurated the venue, setting the tone for what was hoped to be a successful season. The initial buzz was palpable, with a diverse lineup of entertainment slated to follow.

The planned schedule promised a vibrant array of performances, from The Embers to Coors Silver Bullet Band to The Fabulous Kays, The Catalinas, The

Entertainers and the ever-popular Band of Oz. It seemed that the club was destined to be a hotspot on the Myrtle Beach nightlife circuit.

The last known promotion, dated June 8, featured a band called The Blues Other Brothers, a full blues revue similar to the famed Blues Brothers recording stars. The Embers, originally advertised for the week of June 7-10 joined the Band of Oz a week earlier (Jun 2-6). The advertisements in the paper ceased and the future of the club is uncertain.

The end apparently came quietly, with little fanfare. Whether the club survived the summer remains unclear, but its impact was minimal, fading almost as quickly as it had arrived. At one time, a sign from Polo's Lounge & Embers Beach Club was displayed in The North Myrtle Beach Area Historical Museum, a relic of a brief but intriguing footnote in beach music history. The building still stands and became Preston's Seafood Restaurant about 1991.

This brief chapter serves as a reminder of the challenges and unpredictability of the entertainment industry, even for a brand as beloved as The Embers. Despite its short life, the club's legacy lives on, captured in the memories of those who experienced its fleeting charm and the enduring music that continues to define a generation.

On July 17, 1987, The Embers were among a varied selection of North Carolina native musical performers entertaining as part of the U.S. Opening Ceremonies in Raleigh. The event attracted a crowd of 61,000, the largest crowd to that point in the history of Carter-Finley Stadium. Other North Carolina-born artists joining The Embers were Asheville's Roberta Flack and Wilmington's

Charlie Daniels Band. Actor and theater director Ira David Wood directed the elaborate ceremonies broadcast statewide on television.

The Embers also secured a sponsorship with the Ruff Hewn clothing line based in High Point-Greensboro, NC. "Ruff Hewn's rugged and outdoor style fit perfectly with our image," Bobby explains.

In the late summer and fall of '87, The Embers returned to the studio itching to record new music. The last studio encounter was the Christmas LP in 1986, and before that, the "live" Landmark work.

The Embers' influence continued to grow in 1988 with another clothing deal with designer Alexander Julian related to their "Colours" LP and CD. "Alexander Julian's designs were iconic," Bobby says. "His clothing added a new level of sophistication to our look."

The band released the "Colours" LP, featuring the hit song "What You Do To Me," which won Song of the Year at the Third Annual Beach Music Awards at the Myrtle Beach Convention Center.

Notable songs coming from the album included "What You Do To Me" with Craig Woolard on lead and Jackie Gore's lead on "Deeper in Love."

In the late 1980s, The Embers were booked for a party near Jesup, Georgia. Little did they know that this event would spark a lifelong friendship between the band and a group of down-to-earth, fun-loving sponsors.

The Embers were contacted by Jeff Hires, a Jesup attorney, who also had been the lead singer for a popular local band in the 60s called The Chosen Few, which later became The Soul Sensation.

The party occurred at a hunting lodge nestled among the tall pines of Wayne County Georgia, an agricultural hub about fifty miles Northwest of Brunswick. A tight-knit group of local businesspeople, all good friends, decided to throw a bash for their buddies. They dubbed the event a meeting of "The Cooter Ridge Armadillo Hunting Club – Altamaha Chapter," a name that hinted at the laid-back, anything-goes vibe of the evening.

Bobby recalls that night with a laugh. "The first time we ever played for them, I'll never forget it," he chuckled, his eyes twinkling with the memory. "Now, that was one crazy place that night and they had a great turnout."

As the band started playing, the guests sat back, watching, as if sizing up the music. Tomlinson describes it vividly, "Everybody was sitting there watching us. And we started to play, and they all jumped up and converged in the middle of the floor where they made a pile. They were all piled up in the middle of the dance floor doing the gator. It was the funniest thing you've ever seen. Then Jackie's Raymond Massey skit had them rolling in the aisles. They were crazy. I mean, they were, but we played for them for years. It was great."

Among the colorful cast of characters at the heart of this "meeting" was J. William (Bill) Harvey, better known as "Booger," now a retired attorney and city councilman and a proud Sigma Nu alum from the University of Georgia. And there was W.C. Rogers, owner of some local package stores, and Grant Lewis, who ran a lumber company and a towing-recovery business. Also, Mark McGregor, the singing pharmacist from Nahunta, famous in those parts for his soulful renditions of "Smoke Gets in Your Eyes" and "Cowboys to Girls" with his band, the Second Chance Band.

McGregor tells the story of one club meeting when Jackie was walking through the audience singing The

Embers' popular "Jackie Wilson Medley." He said, "Jackie was going from table to table passing the microphone around and stopped at our table while singing 'Lonely Teardrops' and handed the mic to Jack Brinkley."

Brinkley was well-known in those parts as a singer with Mark's Second Chance Band so Brinkley hit all the high notes and the crowd went crazy. After the show, Jackie asked, "Who was that guy?" One of The Embers reminded Jackie that Brinkley was with King David & The Slaves back in the '60s when The Embers opened for them at Myrtle Beach.

Grant Lewis, with his rugged charm and deep roots in Jesup, summed it up best, "We live in the best damn town in the world. We had the best damn music, the prettiest women, and the best cars. And we had The Embers." Those words were the gospel truth to the Jesup crew.

Tomlinson recalled how the bond with these men went far beyond music. "We had played an event down in Fort Lauderdale and had spent the night in Brunswick, Georgia. The next morning, our truck driver called me and said, 'Our truck's broken down.'"

Faced with a potentially disastrous situation, Tomlinson called Grant Lewis. "I explained the situation to Grant and that we were over in Brunswick. He said, 'Don't worry, I'll be there in about an hour.'"

An hour later, Grant pulled up with a wrecker and another tractor. "He said, 'I'll trade my tractor for yours and we'll get your trailer back on the road and my driver is going with you. He'll drop your trailer in Raleigh and return home. I'll get your tractor up to the Freightliner dealer in Savannah and when it's fixed, I'll drop it off for you.' That was Grant Lewis from Jesup."

The Cooter Ridge Armadillo Hunt Club held numerous meetings that included The Embers throughout the 80s and 90s.

Reflecting on the decade, Bobby sees the 1980s as a period of tremendous growth and achievement for The Embers. "The 1980s was our golden era," he says. "We had a strong lineup, incredible fans, and unforgettable experiences. It was a time when everything came together, and we were able to share our love of beach music with the world. Looking back, I'm proud of what we accomplished and grateful for the journey."

The Embers' legacy lives on, reminding us of the timeless appeal of beach music and the power of a great song to bring people together. The golden era of the 1980s was a testament to the band's enduring appeal and their ability to adapt, innovate, and entertain. As ambassadors of beach music, The Embers continued to inspire and delight audiences, proving that the magic of their music is indeed here to stay.

The effects of The Embers' presence in the 1980s can still be observed in the present day. They helped to define what beach music meant for a new era, blending traditional elements with innovation. Their albums from this period continue to be celebrated, and their songs have become classics of the genre. The Embers' ability to adapt while staying true to their roots is a confirmation of their lasting charm and importance in the Carolina Beach Music scene.

This decade was crucial in cementing The Embers' status as legends of the beach music scene, a legacy that continues to influence bands and artists within the genre.

Chapter 29

THE 1990s WAS A TRANSFORMATIVE decade for The Embers. As the new decade began, the music industry was undergoing significant shifts. Cassettes were still being issued by bands and used by consumers and radio deejays. But the digital compact disc, which came into existence in the mid to late 1980s, was now taking over. Bands that had released songs and albums as vinyl and cassette were now evaluating how to move to the new format.

The questions the industry faced were how much of their catalog they reissued and how fast they spent the money to migrate to the new technology. This technological evolution set the stage for a series of changes and challenges that would define the next ten years for The Embers.

They issued their 1988 "Colours" album as a vinyl record and a digital CD. This was the first use of the new format by bands in the Carolinas. The second pressing of the "Colours" album, a Canadian pressing, was the first fully digital beach music CD. "Embracing digital technology was crucial," Bobby explains. "It allowed us to reach a new generation of listeners." It was a good decision, CDs became the "in" thing for over two decades.

The Embers were riding a wave of success that had carried them through the 1980s. Known for their signature blend of rhythm and blues, soul, and rock 'n' roll, they had added disco to their repertoire. "Cheaters Never Win" in 1981 with a brisk tempo was particularly noticeable and became  a staple in the beach music scene. Their high-energy performances and timeless hits solidified their place in the hearts of fans across the Carolinas and beyond.

"Our goal was that we would stay relevant," Tomlinson said.

In 1987, Robert Trammell, a Florida State legislator, booked The Embers for a show at an armory in Tallahassee. The event was a huge success, drawing a packed crowd and marking the beginning of a thirteen-year partnership. Robert, who was chairman of the judiciary in the Florida Legislature, had the influence to bring The Embers back year after year.

The Embers' journey through the Sunshine State began well before the 1990s, but it was in the 90s that they truly established a lasting presence in the state.

Around 1990, Robert Trammell made a surprising discovery. "Robert called me one day," Tomlinson recalled, "and said, 'Bobby, you won't believe this, but I just found out that Bobby Purify is working as a city maintenance custodian at the Tallahassee Municipal Building.'"

Bobby Purify was *the* Bobby Purify of the famous soul duo James & Bobby Purify, known for hits like "I'm Your Puppet," "Wish You Didn't Have To Go," and "Shake a Tail Feather."

Robert was surprised to find such a legendary singer in such an unexpected place and wanted to bring Bobby Purify on stage with The Embers at an upcoming big event in Tallahassee. Tomlinson recalled, "Robert asked me, 'Would you mind if Bobby Purify sang with you?' I couldn't believe it. I said, 'Of course, we'd love that!'"

The Embers already played most of Purify's hits and, with Tomlinson's approval, Robert set out to make it happen. He tracked down Purify at the municipal building and introduced himself, explaining that he was a Florida state legislator and was organizing a big event at the fairgrounds. He told Purify that he had already cleared it with The Embers and asked if he would be willing to sing with them. Purify, who hadn't performed on stage in a long time and mostly sang in church, was hesitant.

But Robert was persistent. He invited Purify to come out to his car and listen to some music before making a decision. "According to Robert," Tomlinson recalled with a smile, "When Robert played one of our CDs, he noticed Purify's foot tapping to the music. Then, suddenly, the man broke out into a big grin and said, 'Them white boys is bad to the bone.'"

Purify agreed to join The Embers for the event and on that night, he took the stage with the band, ready to sing his famous hit, "I'm Your Puppet." Tomlinson said, "Once Purify started singing, we had a hard time getting him off the stage—he didn't want to stop! He was a fantastic singer and that night was something special."

By the late 1980s, The Embers were a household name, their infectious tunes echoing through the airwaves across the nation thanks to a lucrative contract with Budweiser. It was during this high point in their career that they caught the attention of state officials in North Carolina. Dick Trammel, Director of the North Carolina Division of Travel and Tourism, along with his top deputy, David Little, had an ambitious idea that only The Embers could bring to life.

Bobby Tomlinson, the band's steadfast drummer, recalls the initial call. "They were long-time Embers fans and they wanted to talk to me about us doing a commercial for the state of North Carolina." Intrigued by the prospect, Tomlinson agreed to meet with them. Their proposition was enticing but came with a caveat—there was no budget. "Of course, I'd heard that before," Tomlinson chuckled. However, this was their home state and the commercial was to be aired on both television and radio—a tantalizing offer despite the financial constraints.

At that time, The Embers were still riding high with Budweiser, having recently flown to Nashville to record a commercial under the talented producer J.C. Meyers. This connection sparked an idea. Tomlinson proposed a deal. "We'll do it as long as it doesn't cost us anything," he stipulated. "If there are any expenses incurred, you pay them. And whenever it's played on the radio or TV, it should include a tag or footnote saying, 'The Embers for North Carolina Tourism.'" The state officials, eager to proceed but lacking a ready commercial, accepted Tomlinson's terms.

Tomlinson introduced them to J.C. Meyers, who swiftly agreed to craft the commercial. And, miraculously, the state found the money to pay Meyer's fee. "He wrote the commercial and did a great job of it," Tomlinson praised. The resulting piece was a vibrant celebration of North Carolina, capturing the essence of the state from Manteo on the East Coast to Murphy in the far west.

"Whenever people get together, around the Tar Heel State, There's a North Carolina Style in the way we celebrate," the lyrics rang out.

With the script ready, The Embers were flown to Nashville on the Governor's plane to record. The session was a success, producing a song that would soon become synonymous with North Carolina pride. The campaign also included radio commercials and a television video, both emphasizing the theme of celebrating life "North Carolina Style."

The video shoot took The Embers on a whirlwind tour of the state, capturing its diverse beauty and charm. At the zoo in Asheboro, they filmed scenes amidst exotic animals, adding a playful touch as a ball bounced into their midst. In Wilmington, they sailed on a paddleboat along the Cape Fear River, waving cheerfully as the camera rolled. Another memorable scene was shot at the farmer's market in downtown Raleigh, its historic cobblestones providing a nostalgic backdrop for a lively concert. Each location added a unique flavor to the campaign, showcasing North Carolina's rich tapestry of experiences.

Launched in the spring of 1990, the "North Carolina Style" campaign was a hit. The upbeat jingle resonated with audiences.

> "So welcome to the party, we've got a lot to celebrate, we're proud of our country and we're proud of our state, put on your best, put on your best, put on your best North Carolina smile, it's life we're celebrating, North Carolina style."

Tomlinson reflected on its success, noting, "It was really good, and we also got a lot of mileage out of it." The song even found a place on The Embers' 1993 CD, "Feel The Heat," further cementing its legacy.

In 1999, the story came full circle when The Embers were officially recognized as North Carolina's Musical Ambassadors of Goodwill. Tomlinson received a heartfelt letter from Gordon Clapp, then the state's Tourism Director, which encapsulated the band's impact.

> "For years The Embers have been identified with beach music and have brought pleasure to millions of listeners throughout the South and beyond. They truly have become a North Carolina tradition and treasure.
>
> "Their music renews our spirit and brings back vivid images of hot summer nights and cool ocean breezes, and dancing and romancing on the sand with summer sweethearts. Led by original drummer Bobby Tomlinson, they are better than ever, and their popularity continues to grow. We truly recommend and endorse their dependability, character, audience appeal, and of course their music for all ages."

Thus, from a casual phone call to a statewide campaign, The Embers' journey with North Carolina

Tourism was a testament to their enduring appeal and the deep roots they had planted in their home state. Their music, synonymous with joy and celebration, became a cherished part of North Carolina's cultural heritage, a symbol of the state's welcoming spirit and vibrant life.

Chapter 30

The Embers, ever resilient, grapple with personnel changes once more in the 90s. Johnny Barker departs to co-own The Entertainers with Earl Dawkins, while Randy Hignite steps in on keyboards. Hignite, a seasoned musician with notable stints in The Avengers and the Band of Oz, brings his expertise to The Embers, albeit for a brief year-long tenure.

The year 1992 heralds another shift as Andy Swindell replaces Hignite on keyboards. Despite his roots in rock and roll, Swindell swiftly adapts to the rhythmic pulse of beach music. Reflecting the genre's evolution, The Embers introduce Billy Ray Cyrus' "Achy Breaky Heart" into their repertoire, showcasing their ability to blend contemporary hits with classic beach vibes.

Ripete Records reissues three iconic Embers' albums, "I Love Beach Music," "This One's For You," and "25th Anniversary," on CD. The 25th Anniversary CD boasts a special addition with "Buckhead Beach," absent from the original cassette release.

The year 1993 shines brightly for The Embers. They release a promotional four-song sampler for the eagerly anticipated "Feel The Heat" CD during Spring S.O.S. (Society of Stranders). Jackie Gore lends his soulful voice to "I Wanna Be (Your Everything)" and "Fools Rush In," while Craig Woolard takes the lead on "Eveready Man." Newcomer Andy Swindell impresses with his lead vocals on "Ready to Roll."

Later that year, Embers Records released the full CD version of "Feel The Heat," which quickly ascended the charts. Tracks like "Fools Rush In," "I Wanna Be (Your Everything)," and "Love Falling" enjoy prolonged success. The album also features Jackie Gore's evocative lead on "North Carolina Style," a promotional anthem for the state's tourism. Adding a familial touch, "Drowning in the Sea of Love" includes background vocals by Jackie's wife LaRue and daughter Terri Gore infusing the album with a rich, personal resonance.

Ripete Records, recognizing the album's success, reissues it in CD format, cementing its place in beach music history.

The mid-1990s was a period of both triumph and turmoil for The Embers. In September 1994, during an overheated outdoor party in Goldsboro, tensions between Jackie Gore and Craig Woolard erupted on stage, leading to a public attack.

The following is the story as recounted by the band members in the documentary, *The Embers - The Heart* and *Soul of Beach Music*," as told to Skip Crayton and Bill Benners.

John Thompson reflected, "There was a lot of dissension in the band at that time, a lot of egos and stuff."

Johnny Hopkins elaborated, "As you know, with motivated people, there are some high-strung individuals. The whole crowd, I'd say five out of six, were pretty high-strung individuals. They would scream and yell at each other and then forget about it."

H. Lee Brown, the well-known proprietor of Fat Harold's in Myrtle Beach, shared a telling sign of the band's discord, "You knew that they were fighting when you would see five Mercedes come pulling in because every one of them had one. And sure enough, they'd come in there and they wouldn't speak to each other, but when they got on stage, they were a group. They were a family."

Mark Black, who joined the band in 1996, offered insight into their coping mechanisms. "The strangest thing about The Embers, and I tell people this when we get to talking about things like this, the strangest thing is, sometimes when one guy would just get mad with somebody else on the bus or maybe with a whole bunch of us on the bus, that guy would not talk to anybody on the bus for two, three, four weeks. We'd be on the bus together every day for seven days a week, and he just wouldn't speak.

"Some of the other guys' ways of dealing with it would be to just stay quiet. Just be quiet and wait till the bite goes away. Whatever that bite may have been, just go away or get in your bunk and shut up. Don't say anything. Just get in there and just be quiet and do what you do on stage, and on stage, nobody would ever know.

Nobody ever, ever, ever knew what was happening on that bus.

"So, every one of us compartmentalized any problems that we had. At the same time, we were overjoyed with all the happiness that we would have, too, and that would always come out."

The tensions reached a boiling point with Jackie Gore and Craig Woolard, a conflict that encapsulated the internal strife.

Jackie recalled, "Craig Woolard had started playing with the band in 1976. He had always been the number one man in the bands he played with, but in our band, I was the lead singer. Everybody knew who Jackie Gore was, and while Craig was a great talent, his ego clashed with mine. He would make snide remarks about me on the PA system that the audience heard, but usually, I would let it pass. The last job I played with the Embers was at a friend's house in Goldsboro (NC)."

Bobby Tomlinson recalled the scene vividly: "We were playing quite a bit back in those days. We were all over the place. We had driven all night from close to Atlanta to play in Goldsboro on a Sunday for a friend's birthday. Jackie had recorded an album called 'Jackie Gore, Family and Friends.' He wanted to sell it alongside Embers' merchandise, but I thought it would be a conflict of interest. So, he sold it himself during breaks."

Johnny Hopkins described the setting, "We were at this lovely garden party by the lake behind someone's house in Goldsboro. They had a beautiful residence, a swimming pool, pickup trucks filled with ice and beer, and a big crowd of folks who all knew the Embers."

Craig Woolard recounted the pivotal moment, "We were on stage, it was the next to the last song. It was '60-

Minute Man,' with Gerald Davis singing. While Gerald was singing, Jackie called a mutual friend up on stage and started selling him an album. It was the rudest thing I think I've ever seen on stage."

When the song finished, Craig made a comment about Jackie, and Jackie confronted him. "What did you

say on that PA system about me?"

Craig, upset by what he'd seen, responded, "Jackie, if one of us did what you just did, you would be mad as hell."

"At that point," Craig says, "Jackie had his guitar on and moved as though he was going to turn around and leave. Instead, he turned back and swung his guitar neck."

Jackie admitted, "Well, I'd just taken all I could take and I actually struck him on the side of his head with my guitar neck."

Craig described the aftermath, "The tuning pegs went in the side of my head and I was stunned. The next thing I know he has his guitar off and has it like an axe screaming and coming towards me. I still had my saxophone on."

Johnny Hopkins added, "This has never happened. Nobody ever fights, let alone on stage. So, there's guitar necks going like this, and Craig is holding his saxophone up saying, 'Johnny, take my sax. I just got it fixed. I paid a lot of money.'"

Bobby intervened, "I jumped up and came around the front, and we separated them. Many in the audience didn't even know what was going on. I went to the microphone and said, 'ladies and gentlemen, I don't know how we're going to follow that with a song, that's going to be the end of the night.'

"In the dressing room, there were words. Everyone was upset. Jackie left. Craig asked if he should call the police. I said 'No, we're not going to do that. This guy's a friend of ours. We can handle this.'"

The fallout led to a meeting with a mediator. Bobby recalled, "The mediator told us to write down a list of incidents. I had over twenty-five on my list. At the meeting, I said, 'Jackie, we've been playing together for thirty-five years, but I don't think I want to play with you anymore. You've become almost unmanageable.' Everyone else expressed the same desire."

Jackie reacted, "I don't need y'all anyway." Eventually, Jackie, who had been with the band for thirty-four years, left the band, convinced he was The Embers. He told Bobby, "You won't last six months without me."

As part-owner of The Embers, Jackie was awarded a significant financial settlement paid out over nine years.

According to Mark Black, "The Embers took a dive when Jackie left. Jackie Gore was hard to replace."

A decade later, at the 2004 Carolina Beach Music Awards Show, Jackie and Craig made amends. Craig was co-hosting when Jackie walked on stage unannounced and joined him in singing the finale "I Love Beach Music" and the encore "Faraway Places." Craig later joked, "When I first saw him come up, I didn't know if I needed to put on a football helmet or what."

While their harmonious tunes captivated audiences on the stage, behind the scenes, the clashing egos and dissent among the members often threatened the group's unity. These internal conflicts, fueled by personal ambitions and differing visions for the band's future, created a sometimes-turbulent environment that overshadowed their musical achievements.

Chapter 31

Throughout the ups and downs of the 1990s, one constant remained—Bobby Tomlinson. As the original drummer and a founding member of The Embers, Tomlinson was the backbone of the band. His dedication to the music and to the band was unwavering, and he played a crucial role in navigating the challenges of the decade.

Tomlinson's leadership extended beyond his musical abilities. He was a mentor to the new members, helping them integrate into the band and maintain the high standards that fans expected. His experience and steady hand were invaluable as The Embers faced the uncertainties of the 1990s.

In interviews, Tomlinson often spoke about the importance of adaptability and perseverance. He acknowledged the difficulties the band faced but remained optimistic about their future. "The music industry is always changing," he said in a 1998 interview. "But as long as we stay true to ourselves and our fans, we'll continue to thrive."

Despite the challenges, the 1990s were not without their triumphs for The Embers. The band continued to perform regularly, their concerts drawing enthusiastic crowds. Their live shows were a testament to their enduring appeal, with fans old and new flocking to see them perform.

After Jackie Gore's departure, the Embers were busy in late 1994. They would have to settle on a lineup, vocalists, and musicians. The song selection would change significantly and old Embers' standards from their usual sets had to be reinvented.

Don Jordan comes in first on guitar and vocals. He was previously with the country group Southbound Train.

The Embers then brought in Jeff Hayden on sax and vocals. Hayden previously spent time with The Kays, The Entertainers, the Band of Oz, and The Catalinas. His sax parts would allow Craig Woolard to assume more lead vocals. Despite the setback of losing their long-time voice, Jackie Gore, The Embers kept on rolling.

A new Embers single release is included on Ripete's Fall "Ocean Drive '95 sampler" issued at Fall Migration in September 1995. The Embers are in the studio working on a new album. "Did You Boogie With Your Baby" was  included on the Ripete four-song special release as a promotional teaser for their upcoming CD. The song had Jeff Hayden on lead vocals, received significant airplay, and was listed on the year-end beach music chart. Other songs included on the sampler were Lee Dorsey – "Someday" (a 1963 tune), The Raymen – "Baby What You Want Me To Do" (from 1965), and Little Esther Phillips – "Don't Feel Rained On" (1962).

A year after arriving, Don Jordan leaves the band and Bobby goes hunting for another guitar player and calls Jeff Grimes, a close friend from North Carolina.

Jeffrey Miles Grimes was an accomplished musician by the time he hit high school in Nahunta, NC. In the early 70's, he began fill-in work with The Embers and began a long friendship with Bobby, Jackie, and the band. This was during the time The Embers carried two trumpet players and Jeff's saxophone added to the great horn section.

By 1975, Jeff was known in New York City as a guitarist for Atlantic Records and recorded or toured with the likes of The Spinners, The Jimmy Castor Bunch, Ben E. King, Sister Sledge, and more. He returned home in 1978, pursued some original recordings, and was in a band called "10th Avenue," before moving to South Florida to do session work and club bands.

"Bobby was always really good at keeping in touch with his people," recalls Grimes. "He would call every few years when an opening occurred asking 'Are you ready to come home?' He called in 1994 and said 'We got a problem. Jackie and Craig just had a big fight and it looks like we're going to have to hire another guitar player.' But I was tied up with work at the time and I really liked what I was doing when he called.

"But when he called in 1995, I was in a different place. I had been struck by a car and was on crutches with two broken legs. Two of my friends in Miami had been murdered. My house had been broken into, and my neighborhood had gotten really bad," Grimes said. "I was sitting on my couch one night and I hear my car start up. And I open the door and run out the door and my car is driving off down the road.

"So, I'd had about enough of South Florida when Bobby called. I said 'Yeah man, if you can figure out a way to get me up there, I'd love to come with the band, but I'm in a wheelchair. I'm gonna be on crutches for another six months the doctors say. You don't want somebody up there playing guitar on crutches. And Bobby says 'Let me worry about that. I'll send a road crew down there and we'll get a truck and move you back up to North Carolina, and when you get here, you can sit down for as long as you need to get worked into the band.' Bobby made it all happen. He flew the road crew down to Fort Lauderdale, packed me up, moved me out of my apartment, and drove me back to Raleigh."

In November 1995, the multi-talented Jeff Grimes replaced Don Jordan on guitar and added a sax to the band along with a unique voice.

CHAPTER 32

AT THE FIRST Carolina Beach Music Awards in November 1995 at Myrtle Beach, The Embers became the first band to be inducted into The Carolina Beach Music Hall of Fame.

In January 1996, The Embers performed in Washington, DC as part of Bill Clinton's Inauguration as the 42nd President of the United States.

Mark Black, a well-known Charlotte area Appalachian State graduate comes aboard The Embers from The Fabulous Kays as a sax player and singer. The talented musician brings another voice to give Craig a break during their shows.

"My role with the Embers," Mark reported, "to put it crudely, I was an insurance policy. That was my role. They already had Craig Woolard, and he was the main front guy. And Andy Swindell was playing keys and Jeff Grimes was singing and playing guitar and sax. Gerald Davis was playing bass, Bobby was on drums, and Johnny Hopkins was on trumpet. So, my role with the band ended up being an insurance policy when Craig would do three or four songs, and then I would take over and boot it just about as hard as I could go, and that gave Craig some downtime, and then Craig came back and booted it a little longer. And so, we kind of worked the two-headed dragon there for a while.

"I learned how to be meticulous with Gerald Davis and Craig helped shape who I was as a frontman. He helped show me ways not to be timid, but to go after it and be aggressive. And I thought I was until that point. So that changed me. It brought about a lot of notoriety as well. Being who I was as a member of The Embers gave me a lot of external recording jobs that I normally wouldn't get because of who I was and where I was."

On April 10, The Embers released their "Let's Have a Party" album on Ripete Records. The seventeen-song CD is a mix of Carolina Beach Music, Memphis Soul, and Motown. The concept also features the inclusion of several prominent nationally and regionally known star collaborators including Jerry Butler, Jimmy Hall, Maceo Parker, Fingers Taylor, Debbie

Dobbins, Bill Pinkney, Johnny Adams, John Ellison, and Jay Spell.

Among the biggest songs to receive airplay are "Let's Have A Party" by The Embers with Maceo Parker, "Street Corner Serenade" featuring Jimmy Hall, "Bring It On Home to Me" by The Embers with Debbie Dobbins, and a neat "Weekend Medley" with Bill Pinkney that included "TGIF," "Weekend," "Livin' It Up," "Friday Night," "Livin' For The Weekend," and "Party Time Man." It was a major success. Several of the songs charted and The Carolina Beach Music Awards took note.

The Embers' popularity was beginning to attract interest from businesses wanting to be associated with the band. Beer distributors offered co-branded giveaway items such as drink mugs, glasses, and other trinkets.

About 1996, Piggly Wiggly stores and Coca-Cola Classic in the Carolinas were looking for a new advertising angle. Marion Carter, co-owner of Ripete Records of Elliott, SC was approached by Piggly Wiggly. Carter contacted The Embers with another one of those deals they couldn't refuse.

The concept was a promotional CD that would be given away by Piggly Wiggly stores under conditions they determined. So, Carter and The Embers hammered out a deal to share the money. Carter and Ripete would pay the licensing and CD production costs from his half.

Bobby Tomlinson recalled, "The first one we did was a video. We did it down on the beach in a little inlet. It was part of a commercial Piggly Wiggly ran that included Mark Black singing "I Love Beach Music.""

So, a five-song CD of The Embers was released, including a sixty-second bonus, a commercial for Piggly Wiggly mentioning Coca-Cola set to "I Love Beach Music."

Songs on the CD were the original versions of "I Love Beach Music," "Far Away Places," "Canadian Sunset," "I'm Gonna Do Beautiful Things For You," and "Did You Boogie With Your Baby."

One important inclusion on the CD makes it a "must-have" for collectors. Mark Black sings "I Love Beach Music" in the sixty-second commercial. It is the first cover of the song since Jackie Gore's departure.

The CD cover photo featured The Embers' current lineup in tropical shirts taken at the beach with the ocean in the background. Piggly Wiggly and Coca-Cola Classic logos are on the front which is stamped "For Promotional Use Only." The Embers at that time were Bobby Tomlinson, Craig Woolard, Mark Black, Johnny Hopkins, Gerald Davis, Jeff Grimes, and Andy Swindell.

In June, The North Carolina Symphony was paired with The Embers for a "Vivaldi Meets The Embers" musical mixer. The full orchestra accompanied The Embers at a concert in Cary, NC.

The Embers issued the "Embers Live—A Landmark Experience" CD on Ripete, replicating tracks from their Embers Entertainment Enterprises (eEe label) Live LP and Zaymin Live LP. It featured an entire Embers' show at The Landmark Resort Hotel in Myrtle Beach covering over seventy-five minutes and two full-length LPs.

The production also introduces a new player to The Embers' technical works. Keith Houston is credited with digital editing and mastering and his KHP Music distributes the CD for the eEe record label.

Somewhere in the fitness frenzy of the 1990s, as Richard Simmons and Jane Fonda led the charge with their exercise tapes, a different kind of workout routine was making waves. It was a workout to Carolina soul—a beat that could only come from The Embers. But here's the kicker—even The Embers didn't know they were a part of it.

During the fitness craze of the 1990s, while Richard Simmons and Jane Fonda dominated the exercise tape scene, a different kind of workout was quietly gaining popularity. This one had a unique blend of Carolina beach music and California surf music, giving it a distinct rhythm and soul. The twist? Despite licensing several of their tunes, The Embers didn't realize they had become part of this exercise wave sweeping the country.

In the early '90s, as fitness became a booming industry, Atlanta entrepreneur Bruce Blackman, the mastermind behind Sports Music, Inc., saw an opportunity. Blackman, with a musical background, developed audio programs for jogging, aerobics, and walking, designed to keep fitness buffs on pace with catchy tunes. Among the songs he licensed were The Embers' classics "Far Away Places," "Canadian Sunset," and "I Love Beach Music," alongside hits from The Drifters and The Beach Boys.

"It was called *Beach Music Workout*," Blackman recalls. "I put together tapes that started with a slow tempo, picked up the pace, and then cooled you down, all in an hour and a half. Every fifteen minutes, I'd chime in to tell you how many calories you'd burned and how far you'd walked."

But how did Blackman discover The Embers? "I can't remember exactly, but it was probably somewhere along the Mississippi Gulf Coast or in New Orleans. They blew me away, especially Jackie Gore. When I heard him sing 'Canadian Sunset,' I knew we had to make a deal. He's like a male Celine Dion—an incredible voice."

Bobby Tomlinson recalls the deal but admits, "I remember the transaction, but I had no idea what became of it. That one slipped away from us." Indeed, while the tape sold well, it eventually faded into obscurity. No known copies of *Beach Music Workout* on cassette have surfaced, making it a rare collectible for die-hard fans.

While *Beach Music Workout* performed decently, it was Blackman's *Walk to the Marches* that truly took off, with Blackman adopting the character of Master Sergeant Joe Bob Cobb to narrate the tape. "I'd get into character and say, 'Okay, troops, listen up! This is Master Sergeant Cobb, and you know what you have to do—get out there and do it!'"

The success of *Walk to the Marches* and *Beach Music Workout* led to a boom in themed exercise tapes, with Blackman's company producing sixteen different varieties. Blackman inserted the various Embers' songs into several of his various artists exercise series. The *Beach Music Workout* tapes sold well enough to be transferred to CD format in 1996, and one recently surfaced on eBay.

Despite its success, *Beach Music Workout* became a footnote in The Embers' career—largely unknown in the Carolina music scene. Yet, for those lucky enough to stumble upon a copy, they'd be holding a piece of music history—one where The Embers, unknowingly, led a quiet revolution in the fitness world.

As for Bruce Blackman, he's also known as the founder of the band Starbuck, best known for their hit *Moonlight Feels Right*. Interestingly, The Embers covered that very song on their 1976 album *Embers Live in Center Court Lounge*.

Chapter 33

THE 1996 CAROLINA BEACH MUSIC AWARDS was held in November and The Embers racked up four CAMMY's. "Let's Have a Party" was named Best Group Album, Best Collaboration, Best Blues Album, and Best Compilation Album of the Year.

In late 1996 or 1997, Marion Carter of Ripete Records approached The Embers with a concept for a new album. It was a takeoff on the "Stars on 45" mega medleys of the 80s but not what you would have thought. They revisited the timeless smooth swing standards that graced the radio and jukeboxes fifty or more years ago like "September in the Rain," "So Rare," "Canadian Sunset," and instrumentals like "William Tell Overture," as well as other standards.

Gerald Davis was the music director and, working with Marion, stitched together thirty-four magnificent musical standards envisioned as a complete play-through set. For CD release purposes, it was divided into twelve segments. Gerald significantly contributed to many of The Embers' efforts over the years.

"Gerald turned out to be one hell of an audio engineer," said Tomlinson when asked about the CD. "I've never seen anybody quite like him either. He was instrumental in the development of every record we recorded after he joined us. But that forty-five song "String of Pearls"—well, he put the whole thing together. I mean, he pulled together every song. It was really something."

Around Spring Safari in April, The Embers issued a "String of Pearls" Spring S.O.S. special promo release CD. With a limited-run printing, the pale purple CD became a collector's item.

The Embers issued a "String of Pearls" CD on Ripete with two different covers at the end of the year featuring family photos. One other item of note—the songs were recorded at The Embers Sound Emporium in Raleigh. This means that parts of the album were recorded at the home studios of several of The Embers. The drum track was recorded "live" at Red's Beach Music Club.

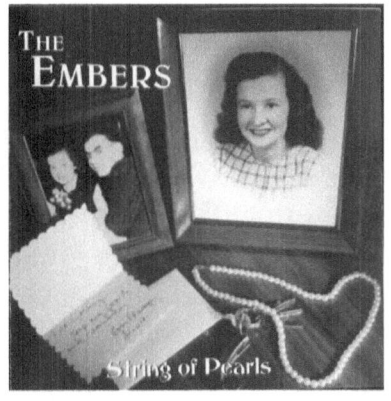

The Jeff Grimes thank you note to his parents in the CD's liner notes said it all: "Your music has become my music." Several of its songs received significant airplay on beach music stations. The "Moonglow/Canadian Sunset/Begin the Beguine Medley" was #29 on the 1997 year-end chart.

The Embers released "Dot Com Your Ass," a single release for the 1998 S.O.S. song CD on Carlen, a secondary Ripete label. The song was a bluesy, upbeat number with lots of computer jargon reflective of the dot com era. The song, written by Cal Duke under a Bill Lowery license, was included in Ripete's "Finger Poppin' Time" Volume II compilation.

In 1998, a new opportunity emerged on the horizon for The Embers. They had an event at one of Randy Watson's parties in Tidewater Virginia. Watson, a personal friend of the Embers, was known to many as a high roller and was a frequent presence in the glittering halls of Atlantic City's casinos. His enthusiasm for The Embers was boundless. "I want to get you guys up to Atlantic City," he would often say, his eyes sparkling with the vision of the band's music echoing through the grand casinos. Initially, Tomlinson, the band's de facto leader, responded with cautious optimism, "You know, maybe."

Months later, Randy called Bobby with a proposal that carried a touch of excitement. "Where are you playing today?" he asked, hinting at a special guest he was bringing along—Charlie Barksdale, of the Sands Hotel and Casino in Atlantic City, who worked closely with the Hotel's big spenders.

That night, The Embers were set to play at NC State University, a venue bursting at the seams with eager fans. "This place was jammed. I mean, you couldn't move, couldn't breathe," Bobby recalled. Randy and Charlie made their entrance as the energy in the room soared. The band had the crowd in a frenzy, their music weaving an electric spell.

During a break, Bobby and the band met Randy and Charlie. "What do you think?" Bobby asked Charlie, who was visibly impressed. "Man, you blew me away," Charlie said. "When can y'all go? We want you in Atlantic City."

What followed was a whirlwind of planning and excitement culminating in an event in 1999 at the Sands Casino. They attracted gamblers and their friends from North Carolina, South Carolina, and Virginia. The weekend featured a packed calendar of activities, including a "pig-picking" and saw people flying in from across the country. "The show went over like gangbusters," Bobby reminisced. "I mean, it was great."

The Embers returned to the Sands Casino the next year, in 2000, for a New Year's Eve performance. "This time, it was different," Bobby noted. "We had a mob that year." The band's performance spanned several days, culminating in a New Year's Eve show that left the audience mesmerized.

As they prepared to leave, Charlie approached Bobby with a last-minute request. "Man, I need you to do me a favor," he said. "I've got a big spender up in the penthouse. It's New Year's Eve, and he wants y'all to come up." Bobby was reluctant at first, "Man, we're ready to roll." But Charlie's insistence won out. "You gotta do it for me," he pleaded. Bobby turned to the band, "Well, guys, we gotta go upstairs for Charlie."

In the penthouse, they found a lavish spread—shrimp, a hundred-year-old bottle of whiskey, and Cuban cigars. The big spender greeted them warmly, expressing his gratitude. Curious, Bobby asked Charlie about the man's identity. "What does he do?" he inquired. Charlie's response was succinct, "Anything he wants to."

Charlie later explained the high-stakes world of the casino, "The only difference between the Yankees and a guy from North Carolina when he comes here," he said, "is when the man from North Carolina loses a hundred thousand dollars, he shakes my hand, and thanks me for a great time. The guy from New York wants to kill me."

Their performance that weekend solidified their reputation. "We really knocked them out," Bobby recalled. The Sands Casino, with its high ceilings and walls adorned with pictures of legends like Dean Martin, Frank Sinatra, Sammy Davis Jr., and Bob Hope, became a place of special significance for the band. The dressing rooms, furnished like elegant living rooms, offered a touch of luxury that made their stay memorable.

Their success led to further collaborations. The Embers returned in the summer to shoot a commercial—a takeoff of "I Love Beach Music." Bobby, always on the lookout for stylish attire, discovered Jams World in Hawaii, where he began sourcing unique outfits for the band. "Most of his clothes were like Hawaiian shirts," Bobby explained, describing the vibrant, baggy, pajama-like pants that became part of their signature look.

The commercial shoot was an elaborate affair. Set in the lobby of the casino amidst giant slot machines they created a memorable visual spectacle. "This slot machine had to pay off every time you pulled it," Bobby said with a chuckle. "I said, 'Well, if you can make it pay off every time, then you can make it not pay off. He said, 'I plead the fifth.'"

Chapter 34

THE COMMERCIAL AIRED NATIONWIDE, and the band's live performance that night was recorded for a live album, "At The Sands Hotel Resort and Casino." Gerald, their musical director, spearheaded the recording using a state-of-the-art 24-track console. The live performance was also filmed, and the resulting VHS tapes and CDs became bestsellers.

Gerald Davis recalled the event this way. "Bobby knew what we were going to do in Atlantic City was a big deal. So, he decided we needed something new to wear and called Jams World in Hawaii and asked them to send us some clothes for a video and commercial we were going to shoot. We'd been ordering stuff from Jam's World for a while. Bobby told them to 'Send me something flashy.'"

When the clothes arrived, Bobby handed them out in clothing bags without looking to see what they looked like. "I carried mine up to my room," Gerald said, "and my wife asked, 'What are you wearing for the video?' I said, 'I don't know. Let me see.' So, I opened the bag and held it up. It was a pair of baggy pink pants—Pepto Bismol pink. And the shirt was a flashy yellow and purple. She said, 'Oh baby.' And I said, 'They told us to get dressed in our room and come down through the casino to the boardwalk. But I can't walk down there with these clothes on.'

"So, I covered the clothes and went down to the casino where we shot the commercial which was called, *'We Love the Sands Casino and the All-New Boardwalk Café.'* We then did a video of the band on the Boardwalk.

"While shooting outside, a mob of people gathered around us and followed us down the boardwalk. And people were looking at us from their hotel rooms. By the time that was over, everybody knew about those pink pants.

"Headed back to the room, I got on an elevator and it was full of people and I still had those clothes on. They stopped talking immediately and when I got off, I could hear him laughing behind me."

Reflecting on the experience, Bobby shared, "It was a really great connection between the two of us. We hadn't played up there in years, but we did that in the early 2000s." The band had indeed left their mark, playing at the casino, starring in a commercial, and recording a live album.

Years later, the band faced a somber moment when Randy Watson passed away. "We were asked to play at his funeral," Bobby said. They set up a few instruments on the porch and played Randy's favorite songs, including "I Love Beach Music." Randy's close friendships with musicians like Ammon Tharp from Bill Deal and the Rhondells were evident as they paid tribute to a man well-respected in the music community.

Randy Watson and Charlie Barksdale had opened doors for The Embers, creating memories that intertwined their lives with the glitz and glamour of Atlantic City.

Meanwhile, The Embers' growing popularity in Florida led to invitations to perform at high-profile political events. One of the most significant of these was the inauguration of Jeb Bush as Governor of Florida in January 1999. The band performed at the Governor's Mansion in Tallahassee in the afternoon shortly after the inauguration.

The crowd consisted of Florida's political elite including the Bush family, former President George H.W. Bush and his son, incoming President George W. Bush.

Gerald Davis recalled, "There were Secret Service agents all around and we were walking around in black suits with the in-ear pieces we use when playing in our ears and people thought we were with the Secret Service. They would look at us and you could read their lips. 'They're with the Secret Service.'"

The event was a major milestone for the band, symbolizing their deepening connection to Florida and their growing influence in the region. From their early gigs in West Palm Beach to their high-profile performances at political events and tailgate parties, The Embers left an indelible mark on the state.

The band was scheduled to perform in Charlotte, NC, at 4 pm the next day. Gerald Davis recalled, "On the way back from the Governor's Inaugural Ball in Boca Raton, before we even got midway in Florida, the bus broke down. We had to be at the Panthers game at 4 o'clock the next day. We *had* to be there. This was about four in the morning and the tractor-trailer equipment truck was about an hour behind us. Bobby said, 'Well, we don't have any choice. We've got to get there. Maybe we can ride in the truck.'

Only one of us could sit in the cab with the drivers, so I grabbed my little thin mattress out of my bunk and took it with me as we climbed in the back of the truck. I made a bed on top of a PA cabinet. I didn't realize how bouncy that road along Interstate 95 could be. Being in the back of a tractor-trailer was really bad bouncing around on that equipment.

"It's probably about a 12-hour drive. We had no way to communicate with our drivers because we didn't carry our cell phones with us. If you had to go to the restroom, you were pretty much up the creek until they decided to stop. And it got colder and colder and colder as we headed north.

"By the time we got to Charlotte, it was about twenty degrees outside. We pulled up at the stadium, and there was a bunch of people out there waiting for the pregame party.

"They came and pulled up to the back of the truck, and we all jumped out of the back of that tractor-trailer, looking road-worn, sleepy, and tired. That's not the only time we'd had to ride in the back of the truck.

"We had to ride in the back of the truck several times because the motto there is, 'the show must go on.' You get to the job whatever you have to do."

As the 1990s came to a close, The Embers had solidified their place as one of the most beloved bands in Florida. Their journey through the state was about connecting with people, building relationships, and creating moments that would be cherished for years to come. The Embers' Florida connection remains a shining example of how music can transcend boundaries and bring joy to all who experience it. Whether at a gubernatorial inauguration, a college basketball game, or The World's Largest Tailgate Party, The Embers were there making memories that would last a lifetime.

The decade culminated in 1999 with The Embers being named North Carolina's Official "Musical Ambassadors of Good Will." This designation was a fitting tribute to their contribution to the state's musical heritage and their role in spreading the joy of beach music far and wide.

In August 1999, The Raleigh News and Observer published its take on the state's top influencers in the 1900s. The article included an extensive list of contributors to state history. The paper stated:

> In the past century, The Embers band was the only one single outpouring of contributions to our culture. They have continued to perform throughout the Tar Heel State, the South, and elsewhere in North America and have been truly a musical ambassador for our state.
>
> Their programs always contain material that plugs the many virtues of North Carolina as a great place to visit. Several years ago, their association with the state was reinforced when they recorded special songs that helped us publicize North Carolina via personal appearance and by recording customized music, and public service announcements for radio and television stations. While under contract with the Division of Tourism, Film, and Sports Development, there again would be a call to make new spots that would extol the virtues of vacationing here, as well as

performance functions that would help promote our state.

Although there are other musical groups based in our state, none have attained the level of recognition that The Embers have in representing the state of North Carolina as musical ambassadors of goodwill throughout our continent.

Twenty-one individuals or organizations were listed as the Creators—Artists and Inventors Whose Work Shape Our State and The Nation's Perception.

The Embers were included along with notable creators such as Ava Gardner, Neil Young, Andy Griffith, John Coltrane, Doc Watson, and Arthur Wilson. Sarah Avery, a staff writer for the paper at the time, penned the feature on The Embers.

The Embers sound was the beach. The sound spread along the sandy shores of North and South Carolina as an outgrowth of racial climate that made rhythm and blues risqué for white audiences unless it was performed by white musicians and played in the heady freedom of beach dance clubs.

By the 1950s, beach music had taken over like kudzu. For a group of kids in the Broughton High School marching band, the dance-inducing sound inspired them to put together a beach music ensemble for a talent show in Cameron Village.

By 1958 they called themselves The Embers and took off for the beach—Ocean Beach, Carolina Beach, and Atlantic Beach, where they eventually opened their second Embers Club at the circle in the center of town.

In one incarnation after another, only the original member - Bobby Thomlinson - remains. The Embers have come to be unequivocally and quintessentially associated with beach music. Say beach music, think The Embers. The group's 1979 hit, I Love Beach Music, defines the genre.

Although the group no longer operates its own clubs, members still perform to crowds, and not just the tassel loafer and Madras shirt set. Among the group's

staunchest fans are college students who know all the lyrics to their songs.
—*The Raleigh News and Observer*

The 1990s was a decade of resilience and reinvention for The Embers. From significant personnel changes and internal conflicts to national recognition and innovative releases, the band navigated the challenges with determination and creativity. Bobby Tomlinson's steadfast leadership and the collective talent of the band members ensured that The Embers remained a beloved fixture in the beach music scene.

As they moved into the new millennium, The Embers carried with them the experiences and lessons of the 1990s, ready to continue their legacy as pioneers of Carolina Beach Music.

CHAPTER 35

AS THE 2000s BEGAN, The Embers continued to hold the prestigious title of "North Carolina's Official Musical Ambassadors of Good Will." This designation was in recognition of their enduring popularity and influence in promoting the culture and charm of the Carolinas.

The 2000s was a decade of resilience and reinvention for The Embers. From significant personnel changes and internal conflicts to national recognition and innovative releases, the band navigated the challenges with determination and creativity. Bobby Tomlinson's steadfast leadership and the collective talent of the band members ensured that The Embers remained a relevant fixture in the beach music scene.

By May 1, 2000, the North Carolina Department of Tourism, Film, and Sports Development signed a contract with The Embers. The agreement detailed a series of performances and recordings, beginning with a performance on May 10, 2000, at the State Capitol grounds for the Interagency Tourism Fair. The band was also slated to perform at the Fourth of July celebration in

Ottawa, Ontario, Canada, and to record musical backgrounds for various public service announcements.

On July 4, 2000, The Embers embarked on an extraordinary journey to Ottawa, Canada, organized by North Carolina Tourism and Economic Development. Piedmont Airlines provided a charter plane filled with the state's governor, dignitaries, and a bounty of Carolina cuisine. Bill's Barbecue, a Wilson landmark, sent a truck ahead to have fresh-cooked North Carolina vinegar-style barbecue ready for the event.

The trip began early in the morning with the plane buzzing with excitement. Upon arrival in Canada, the delegation was swiftly taken to a downtown hotel and greeted with a lavish meal. That day, the band, including their sound man Terry Garrett, gathered their bags and headed to the U.S. Ambassador's residence, a magnificent venue perched on a hill overlooking the convergence of two rivers.

The guest house at the Ambassador's residence was well-prepared with food, changing rooms, and all necessary amenities for the band. They set up their equipment and conducted a sound check, all while the Royal Mounted Police and their dogs ensured security. A humorous moment unfolded when the police dogs alerted to a bag, only to discover it contained two McDonald's Big Macs, much to Terry's amusement.

During the sound check, Governor James B. Hunt mingled with the band, warmly greeting Bobby Tomlinson and others. The atmosphere was vibrant and friendly as they prepared for the evening's performance.

As people began to arrive, Bobby took a moment to check the stage. He was approached by a man in khaki pants, a blue oxford cloth shirt, and a Panama hat, who introduced himself as Gordon Giffin, the American Ambassador. Giffin shared a nostalgic story of how he and his wife, both Duke University alumni, had frequented The Embers Club during their college days and had always dreamed of having The Embers perform at a private party. This dream had now come true.

The performance was a grand affair, attended by notable figures including Canadian Prime Minister Jean Chrétien. The Embers delivered their regular show, including a lively second set where Craig invited guests to join him in dances like the swim, the twist, and the funky chicken. Among those who took part were the Prime Minister, his wife, the Ambassador, and his wife, all dancing the funky chicken.

The day was a resounding success, thanks to The Embers' enduring charm and the strong ties they had forged with North Carolina and beyond.

Ambassador Giffin remembers the event this way, "The Embers have been a part of my life since 1967. The time we had the band in Ottawa was enormous fun. The newspapers the next day reported that when I came up on the stage, whoever in the band had the mic (Craig Woolard) said, 'You all may know him as Mr. Ambassador, but we know him as the Party Animal,' I couldn't stop laughing."

The year 2001 saw The Embers venturing into new territories while also receiving significant recognition for their contributions to music. They released "Live at the Sands," a VHS of their performance at the Atlantic City, NJ Casino Resort, accompanied by a CD of the music from that memorable night.

During this time, Randy Watson, a Tidewater, Virginia businessman with automobile and food catering businesses, and Charlie Barksdale, the PR guy from The Sands, played a role in promoting the release. However, the constant change in the band's lineup continued, particularly with the keyboards. Freddy Tripp, who had previously played with The Breeze Band, Band of Oz, and The Fantastic Shakers, was brought on to fill the role.

In recognition of their contributions to the genre, The Embers was named to the South Carolina R&B/Beach Music Hall of Fame. Additionally, Bobby Tomlinson was honored with the Joe Pope Pioneer Award by the Carolina Beach Music Awards (CBMA), celebrating his dedication and pioneering spirit in beach music.

Chapter 36

IN 2001, Craig Woolard, now established as lead vocalist for The Embers and known for his rich, soulful vocals, wanted something new. Teaming up with Chris Biehler, owner of Forevermore Records, Woolard recorded a cover of "Love Don't Come No Stronger (Than Yours and Mine)," as a solo artist on Biehler's label. The track became a standout in Woolard's career, showcasing his ability to blend emotion with a strong beach music groove. It was included on the Forevermore compilation CD "This is Beach Music Volume II" and Woolard's song was a chart-topper.

Meanwhile, The Embers continued working with Randy Watson on a new project to captivate Craig's song title and came up with The Embers "With Love" CD. All the songs on the CD featured "love" themes. The Embers licensed Woolard's big hit, "Love Don't Come No Stronger," from Chris Biehler and another strong album on eEe was the result. Two of the songs on the CD were produced by Mark Black and Freddy Tripp.

Bobby and Charles Wallert renewed acquaintances February 28-March 3, 2002 at the Association of Beach and Shag DJ's 11th Annual "DJ Throwdown" at Myrtle

Beach. Tomlinson was there with The Embers, who performed that weekend. Wallert, an artist-producer, was there promoting some of his recent recordings that fit the beach music genre.

Wallert and Tomlinson first met in November 1988 at the Third Annual Beach Music Awards in Raleigh. The Embers were named Group of the Year and Jackie Gore won Entertainer of the Year and Group Vocalist of the Year. Meanwhile, Wallert and O.C. Smith's song "Brenda" won Best Club Song, Best Classic Song, and Smith was named Male Vocalist of the Year.

"He was there that night in 2002 and we talked," recalled Tomlinson. I had heard about O.C. Smith's passing the year before and had called Wallert to express my condolences. And then I ran into him at Myrtle Beach. And he said, 'We need to get together and talk about recording you guys.' So, we talked and got together and came up with a plan. He already owned Bluewater Records. Of course, we had Embers Entertainment Enterprises. So, I decided to partner with him, and within a few months, efforts were underway for a new CD."

Wallert, a producer-songwriter, had the idea to bring together several of the nationally known artists he worked with including Smith, Cuba Gooding, George Benson, and others along with The Embers to make a super collaboration of great beach music songs. The initial recording session was held in New York in the Fall.

That Fall, Kevin White, a theater musician from Virginia who had worked with national artists, replaced Freddy Tripp on keyboards and The Embers have a solid band again.

In 2003, Woolard would team up with 19-year-old Marsha Hancock, an Oxford, NC native, who sought his help with a school project. The two joined voices for a cover of Smokey Robinson's huge 80s hit "Cruisin'." It, too, became quite popular on the beach music charts and was included on Ripete Records' various artists compilation "Beach Party II." Marsha would be a contestant on American Idol in 2007.

The Embers trekked to New York twice to work on what would be their nineteenth album. A two-song Bluewater teaser CD was released for S.O.S. in April. It featured Craig Woolard on lead singing Wallert's "Beach Music" and "We Made Them Dance" which was well received.

April 27, 2003, marked the 10th Anniversary Awards Show by the Rhythm-N-Blues Network in the program, "*A Tribute to O.C. Smith from The Embers.*" During this event, The Embers released the single "Beach Music/We Made Them Dance" with its cover, adding another milestone to their storied career.

The Embers' role as North Carolina's Ambassadors of Tourism placed the band at a prestigious historical commemoration December 12-17, 2003. State and Federal dignitaries, including President George W. Bush, gathered at Kitty Hawk on the Outer Banks to commemorate the 100th Anniversary of the Wright Brothers' historic flight.

As 2004 arrives, The Embers are working hard with Wallert for their upcoming album when Kevin White leaves. The loss is compounded in March when Craig Woolard departs over a contract dispute. Jerry Tellier, a proven Broadway singer, comes in to share lead vocal duties with Mark Black. Woolard's previous vocal work on the album would need to be reworked.

Tellier brings his experienced voice to The Embers. He had singing roles in Broadway's "Smokey Joe's Café," "Saturday Night Fever," and "42nd Street." He picks up the beach style and, in May, after S.O.S., a four-song teaser, "The Embers Beach Music Super Collaboration Sampler," was released. It features Mark Black and Tellier on re-recorded versions of "Beach Music" and "We Made Them Dance" and two other songs from the upcoming album.

The new album was officially released after S.O.S. in

2004 entitled "The Embers Beach Music Super Collaboration." The Embers are featured on eight of the fifteen songs on the album and collaborate with others on two other songs. Most of the songs are Wallert compositions and feature artists Wallert had worked with in the past. "Beach Music" and "We Made Them Dance," featuring a nifty guitar solo by Jeff Grimes, received airplay in the Carolinas with "Beach Music" reaching #22 on John Hook's Beach Music Top 40 in 2004.

With a new solid band, The Embers obtained a new Pepsi sponsorship that included a tour that highlighted their status.

The constant flux of band members continued in 2004. Donnie Weaver, from The O'Kaysions' "Girl Watcher" fame, replaced Kevin White on keyboards and vocals from February to August, leaving after an auto accident. Durwood Martin, Andy Swindell, and Johnny Barker filled in temporarily during this period.

By August 2004, The Embers found themselves at another turning point. Mark Black, their dedicated sax player and vocalist, after nine years with the band, wanted to spend more time with his family and take a job teaching which created a significant vacancy in the band.

Known for their lively performances and soulful melodies, The Embers needed a new member who could seamlessly fit in—a horn player with vocal talent. The word spread quickly through the music community, sparking a search for fresh talent to join their ranks.

"It was Jerry Polk, a cherished friend of The Embers from Charleston and drummer for the East Coast Party Band, who reached out to me with a promising recommendation," Bobby remembered. "Polk had a keen eye for talent, understood what I needed, and suggested I contact Wayne Free."

Wayne had spent nearly a decade with The Swinging Medallions, a band who, like The Embers, was also known for its vibrant performances. "Wayne had left The Swinging Medallions and settled in Charlotte," Polk told Bobby. "And he was disenchanted with his current situation."

Intrigued, Bobby contacted Wayne. "We're in a bind," Bobby admitted to Wayne. "We have a gig in Virginia and need a second singer with a horn to come on board and sing ten songs to get us through this Virginia booking."

Known for his skill with both the trumpet and trombone, Wayne saw this as a chance to be part of a legendary band. Arrangements were quickly made for Wayne and Gerald Davis, The Embers' music director, to coordinate the details for Wayne's first performance with the band.

Wayne met the bus in Burlington, North Carolina, where he and Gerald spent time on the bus selecting songs for the show and working out the arrangements on the way to the performance.

That night, on stage, his first notes blended effortlessly with the band's sound, and his vocals added a new dimension to their music. Songs like "Far Away Places" and "I Love Beach Music" were brought to life in a fresh way. The audience responded positively, and Wayne's fellow band members were impressed. After Wayne filled in for Mark several more times, Bobby asked him to join the band full-time.

Wayne's presence was more than just filling a vacancy, he brought new energy and talent as a key member of The Embers from 2004 to 2014. His voice was featured on the album "The Show Must Go On," adding depth to the band's music. His influence extended beyond performances as he took on the role of music coordinator, helping to shape the band's sound. Wayne's contributions included hits like "Little Mama," "Lovey Dovey," "It Ain't the Meat (It's the Motion)," "Hook, Line, and Sinker," and "Besamé Mucho" in 2012.

In addition to his musical contributions, he assisted Bobby with driving duties, sharing the responsibility of transporting the band to their numerous gigs. His dedication to The Embers was evident, and his impact on the band was significant.

CHAPTER 37

PERSONNEL CHANGES remained a constant theme in 2005. Despite the shifts, The Embers continued to produce new music, releasing the "Christmas with The Embers" CD on the Bluewater label. This festive album captured the spirit of the season, blending traditional holiday tunes with The Embers' unique beach music style.

In 2006, Stephen Pachuta joined the band on trumpet and background vocals, bringing a new dynamic to their performances. Josh Shilling also joined on keyboards and vocals, though his tenure lasted only from June to December. These additions reflected the band's commitment to evolving their sound and maintaining their high-energy performances.

During the summer of 2006, Piggly Wiggly reached out once again. This time, the grocery chain entered into a sponsorship with The Embers to perform eight or ten concerts at specific store locations as part of a promotional campaign titled "Piggly Wiggly Presents The Embers."

At that time, The Embers' lineup included Wayne Free, Bobby Tomlinson, Gerald Davis, Jerry Tellier, Josh Shilling, Jeff Grimes, and Stephen Pachuta. Throughout

the summer, the band members sported various colored T-shirts emblazoned with the iconic Piggly Wiggly pig on the front. They traveled to different Piggly Wiggly store locations, playing free concerts in the parking lots. The events were well-advertised, attracting substantial crowds.

The year 2007 was significant for The Embers, marked by the release of "Vintage Embers 1958-1969," a greatest hits CD on Ripete. This release was a celebration of their long and storied career, offering fans a nostalgic journey through their early recordings.

The CD sold well. It was also very significant due to the fact it included several tunes that were contained on the 1960s unreleased Lucky 13 album recorded at JCP Studios in 1966 or 1967. Keith Houston at KHP Records handled the remastering. Songs that were released for the first time included the following Embers' covers: "I've Been Hurt," "Hey Baby," "Oo Poo Pah Doo," "May I," and "Call Me."

Still, turnover continued to be a theme. Josh Campbell joined from The Swinging Medallions on bass, Jonathan Kuehling was hired on keyboards from February to April, and Clay King came on board as a saxophonist and vocalist.

In another highlight, The Embers released "The Show Must Go On," a one-hundred-print promo on Bluewater. This album underscored their resilience and determination to continue making music despite the ongoing changes.

Debbie Mack, a former member of the Big John Band, joined on keyboards and vocals, becoming the first full-time female musician in the band's history. David Dixon also joined on guitar, adding to the rich tapestry of The Embers' sound.

The Embers returned to the studio working on a second Bluewater album. A limited-edition preview release of the twelve-song album "The Show Must Go On" was released on June 22, 2007. The final version of the album, The Embers' second Bluewater album, was released in August 2008. Wallert is listed as producer and Dr. Bill Ballance as executive producer. The CD showcases Jerry Tellier on lead vocals on "Lovin' On Borrowed Time" among others. Wayne Free is the lead on "The Show Must Go On," "Never Give Up," "I've Done Things With You," and "Wastin' My Love On You."

Debbie Mack departed and was replaced by Ricky Sanders on keyboards and sax player Clay King left for the band On The Rocks. Despite ongoing personnel changes, The Embers pressed on.

Tellier left the band in December 2008 and Wayne Free became the frontman and lead singer for the Embers. Johnny Barker returned to The Embers shortly afterward to replace Donnie Weaver, who had been seriously injured in a car accident.

John Ray joined on bass and, once again, The Embers entertained U.S. troops in Korea at Christmas, their second time performing for the troops.

The release of "Christmas with The Embers" on Pres-Jax, featuring music from their Embers Christmas Show and "I Love Christmas Music," further solidified their reputation as purveyors of festive cheer.

As the decade drew to a close, The Embers continued to embrace new opportunities and evolve their lineup. Matt Kosma joined on saxophone, replacing Clay King, and the band released "I Love Christmas Music" on Pres-Jax.

Throughout the 2000s, The Embers faced numerous challenges and changes, yet their commitment to their music and their fans never wavered. They continued to be ambassadors of beach music, spreading joy and nostalgia wherever they performed. The Embers' experiences and lessons of the 1990s were emblematic of The Embers' approach to music and life. "We never just went somewhere to play a gig and leave," Bobby reflected. "We made friends everywhere we went. Those friendships, those bonds we created—they're still here today."

Their music became the soundtrack to countless memories, and their legacy continues to live on in the hearts of those who danced, sang, and celebrated with them.

Chapter 38

OVER THE DECADES, the holiday season became a crescendo of chaos and joy for bands across the country, and The Embers were no exception. This period transformed into a whirl of festive fervor, with private Christmas parties and corporate events filling up their calendar, each gig paying handsomely.

With Raleigh close to the Research Triangle Park, a hub of innovation and enterprise, The Embers often found themselves at grandiose celebrations, bathed in twinkling lights and holiday cheer. Yet, the early 2000s brought an unexpected chill. The economic downturn and shifting corporate policies cast a shadow over this once-thriving season, and the demand for holiday bands waned.

Myrtle Beach, however, offered a beacon of hope. For years, it had been a sanctuary of Christmas magic with the Alabama Theatre's Christmas Show reigning supreme. Opening just before Thanksgiving and running through to New Year's, these shows captivated audiences with their splendor. It was here that Bobby Tomlinson found inspiration.

"I said, 'Why don't we do a poor man's version of one of those shows and put it on the road?'" Tomlinson reminisced. "We already knew how to do floor shows, so we came up with a Christmas Show starting in 2004."

The Embers' repertoire included all the beloved Christmas standards including "Jingle Bells," "Rockin' Around the Christmas Tree," "White Christmas," and Burl Ives' "Holly Jolly Christmas."

One of the highlights of their performances was the inclusion of "Let It Snow, Let It Snow, Let It Snow." They bought machines that blew fake snow, creating a magical winter wonderland on stage.

"My family always got into Christmas and I happened to have a plush Santa Claus suit," Bobby noted. "We would play Christmas songs, do a few comedy spots and, close to the end, I would put on this Santa Claus outfit and come out and play, which was always a hit.

"We used to do twenty to twenty-five shows each year. We'd start around Thanksgiving. It wasn't just Friday or

Saturday. We did them every day of the week," Tomlinson said, reflecting on the frantic pace of their holiday season.

Each performance was a tapestry of holiday magic, woven with threads of music, laughter, and tradition. The plush Santa Claus suit became a symbol of their journey, embodying the spirit of Christmas that they shared with countless audiences. The fake snow machines, the garland and lights, the heartfelt renditions of beloved carols—all of these elements came together to create an unforgettable experience.

Tomlinson's leadership and vision were the guiding stars of this festive voyage. His ability to adapt and innovate kept The Embers relevant and beloved, even as the landscape of holiday entertainment shifted. Their success was not just measured in ticket sales and full houses, but in the joy and memories they created for their audiences.

The Embers' Christmas Show became more than a performance, it became a tradition. Families returned year after year, children grew up watching Santa Claus play the drums or the saxophone, and communities looked forward to the arrival of the holiday season, heralded by The Embers' Christmas music. Tomlinson's dream of creating a "poor man's version" of the Myrtle Beach spectacle had blossomed into a beloved holiday institution.

As the years went by, the essence of their Christmas Show remained unchanged. It was a celebration of everything that made the season special—the music, the laughter, the decorations, and the sense of togetherness. Tomlinson's passion for Christmas, evident in every detail of the show, was infectious. "We were able to take the show on the road," he said, his voice filled with satisfaction. "And they're still doing it."

In 2007, as The Embers were showcasing their Christmas production, the band received an email from the Army. General Aycock had expressed a keen interest in bringing their Christmas show to the troops stationed overseas. Initially unaware of Aycock's promotion, Bobby was swiftly enlightened by a mutual friend that their Goldsboro friend had been promoted to General and stationed in Korea. With the contact details in hand, Bobby made the call overseas and discussed the possibility of bringing their show to the troops.

"And it was like everything else," Bobby said, "they've got everything but money. 'But it won't cost you anything,' the General said. How could we say no? Of course, we would do it."

Over the course of five days, they visited five different military bases, each hosting a diverse audience comprising both American troops and Korean personnel. The routine was consistent. Picked up in the morning, transported to a base, and provided with all necessary equipment by a Korean road crew.

The first base where they performed was home to a staggering 10,000 troops. Adjustments had to be made to their usual show format, as the presence of the General required a different closing sequence. Instead of the customary bow and curtain closing, they remained in place for the General's address.

"The base General would come up and award us a plaque commemorating our being there. And every General has his own medal that was a little bigger than a silver dollar with their base and their name on it. And they would give each one of us a medal and shake our hand and thank us for doing what we did."

The response from the troops was overwhelmingly positive. Despite the grueling schedule and unfamiliar surroundings, they delivered their best performances, drawing in soldiers with their familiar tunes and infectious energy. The troops, far from home and family, found solace and connection in the music of their homeland.

After each show, Bobby and the band would meet with the audience, selling Christmas CDs and engaging in conversations with the soldiers. It was heartwarming for Bobby to witness the soldiers' eagerness to connect with them, many expressing gratitude for the taste of home their music provided.

The whirlwind week was grueling. Within five days, they covered the entirety of South Korea, including a trip to the southernmost base. However, plans to visit the northernmost point fell through due to escalating tensions at the border.

Their experience on the bases was eye-opening, with tanks scattered around serving as a stark reminder of the military presence in the region.

Reflecting on their time in Korea, Bobby said, "It was something I'll never forget. And there was never a second thought when General Aycock contacted us to do it again in 2008. Of course, we did."

Chapter 39

THE MUSIC BUSINESS, ever a capricious beast, thrives on change. The early 2010s were no different for The Embers, Raleigh's heralded purveyors of beach music. As technology evolved, automobiles flaunted USB ports, leaving cassette decks in the dust and questioning the future of CD players. This era of transformation mirrored the shifts within The Embers, a band always in tune with the pulse of progress.

In 2010, The Embers gifted their fans with "Merry Christmas from The Embers 2010," a holiday treat released on Pres-Jax. Despite the relentless march of time and technology, their commitment to their audience remained steadfast. Meanwhile, The Legends of Beach, a group of former Embers, dissolved, prompting the return of Jeff Grimes to the fold. Grimes, with his mastery of guitar, saxophone, and vocals, brought a seasoned edge back to The Embers.

By 2012, the band welcomed Jimmy Weaver to their ranks. Weaver, a keyboard virtuoso with a voice to match, had previously played with The Castaways and with Steve Owens and Summertime. His arrival added a fresh, yet familiar melody to The Embers' harmonious ensemble. The following year saw the addition of Hugh "Tuff" Blanton, a bass player with roots deep in Monroe, North Carolina. Blanton's tenure with Earl Dawkins' Entertainers and Dink Perry's Breeze Band infused The Embers with his rich, resonant rhythms.

A pivotal moment unfolded in the fall of 2013. Bobby Tomlinson, the heartbeat of The Embers, along with his sponsor Dr. Bill Ballance, yearned to rekindle the magic with a former Ember. Bobby recounts this serendipitous event with vivid clarity, "As luck would have it, we had a night off. Jeff Grimes ventured out to catch The Craig Woolard Band. Craig had brought his children along and, as fate would have it, they ran up and embraced Jeff, who inquired, 'How's the band doing?' Craig's kids replied, 'Great.'

"Then, one of Craig's children suggested, 'You ought to get Daddy to come back. He wants to play with you again if you ask him.' And thus, a spark was ignited."

Bobby and Dr. Ballance met with Craig, and after six months of heartfelt negotiations, a deal was struck. In March 2014, Craig Woolard made his triumphant return to The Embers. After leading The Craig Woolard Band for a decade, Craig resumed his role as lead vocalist and saxophonist, with his name emblazoned on the marquee. It was now officially "The Embers featuring Craig Woolard."

Alongside him came Andy Swindell on keyboards and Bobby Nance on trumpet and valve trombone. Nance, having played with Novas IX and The Catalinas, added layers of depth and brass to the band's evolving sound.

"Craig came back at a good time for us," Tomlinson mused. "We needed another boost, and Craig sure gave us one."

April 2014 saw the release of McBryde Films' two-hour documentary DVD, *"The Embers - The Heart and Soul of Beach Music,"* capturing the essence of the band's legacy, as told by current and former members of the band going all the way back to their beginning.

Accompanying the documentary was a music CD featuring songs that resonated with the band's storied history, pieces of which were speckled throughout the documentary.

In 2014, after a decade of dedication, Wayne Free left The Embers to explore new opportunities.

Also in 2014, Bobby and Jackie buried the hatchet. Bobby explained, "The Embers were booked in Kenansville, for a big event in their Events Center. This was at the time Craig Woolard was returning to the band but he and Andy Swindell had a final event with The Craig Woolard Band.

"Wayne Free was gone so I called the guy who booked us to see if we could reschedule. He said they booked The Embers and wanted The Embers as they had spent a lot of money to advertise it.

"So, I contacted Durwood to play keyboards and called Jackie. He agreed to come. Kenansville pretty much had the original Embers that night.

"But that day, when we got there, Jackie was already there. He was singing. I hadn't spoken to him since we parted. He hugged me and said, 'I would have never done you like you did me.' I replied, 'I will never put you in the position that you put me in.' We played several jobs together since then.

"You know, time heals a lot of things. If you don't speak, you don't cause confrontations. It eventually will work itself out."

The accolades continued to pour in during 2014 and on October 16, The Embers were inducted into the North Carolina Music Hall of Fame, sharing the honor were luminaries like Link Wray, Talmadge "Tab" Smith, Clay Aiken, and the posthumous "Little Eva" Boyd of "Locomotion" fame.

The Embers are also members of the South Carolina Rhythm and Blues Hall of Fame and the South Carolina Beach Music Hall of Fame.

By February 2015, Bobby Tomlinson stood as the last original member of the band that ignited in Raleigh in 1958. The lineup now included Stephen Pachuta, whose talents spanned trumpet, vocals, and keyboards, David Dixon on guitar, John Ray on bass, Matt Kosma on saxophone, and Rick Sanders on piano. In November, a new lineup was on stage as The Embers featuring Craig Woolard was crowned Carolina Beach Music Group of the Year.

Chapter 40

IN THE SPRING OF 2016, The Embers received an unusual request, one that would lead them into an unforgettable experience. Bobby Tomlinson recalls this momentous event vividly as if it were yesterday.

"Someone called on behalf of T.J. Lubinsky, the well-known Public Broadcasting Service host," Bobby begins, his eyes lighting up at the memory. "Lubinsky had an offer that The Embers simply couldn't refuse. He was planning a national PBS program to examine beach music from both the East and West Coast perspectives and wanted The Embers to join the fun.

"Bands to be included were The Beach Boys, Ken Knox and the Chairmen of the Board, Jan and Dean, The Embers featuring Craig Woolard, and for The Embers to back up Ammon Tharp on a Bill Deal and the Rhondells' Medley. A few other bands were also part of this star-studded line-up.

Lubinsky's vision was grand. He aimed to create a special program that highlighted the rich, diverse tapestry of beach music, capturing its essence from coast to coast. "He wanted us to do the special. He was going to fly us to Pittsburgh, record us, and fly us back home. It would be a long day, leaving at 9 A.M., returning by midnight," Bobby recounts, emphasizing the whirlwind nature of the plan.

When the day arrived, "We flew into the Pittsburgh airport," Bobby says, the excitement still palpable in his voice. Upon arrival, they were each handed a flat fee of one thousand dollars. "One thousand dollars!" Bobby exclaimed. "A flat fee to come up and do three songs," he added, nodding his head as if still marveling at the simplicity yet generosity of the arrangement.

As they disembarked at Pittsburgh Airport, they met Ammon Tharp there. "And they sent two limousines to pick us up," Bobby continues, painting a picture of luxury and anticipation. They all had the impression that they were heading to a recording studio.

"But we rode and rode. We rode for about an hour," he says, a chuckle escaping as he remembers their growing confusion. "All of a sudden, we go into a fairly high-end neighborhood," Bobby recalls, still puzzled by the unexpected turn of events.

The limousines stopped in front of a large gate at a cul-de-sac. Bobby couldn't help but think, "What the hell is a studio doing here?" The gate opened to reveal a mansion eerily familiar to Bobby and his bandmates. "Do you remember Dark Shadows?" Bobby asked, his face lighting up with recognition. "It used to be on TV. They did twelve hundred episodes," The mansion before them was a replica of the one from Dark Shadows. "I mean it was just like it. It was as if they picked it up and put it there," he marveled.

The cars pulled up to the mansion and their instruments and clothing were swiftly taken by a flurry of attendants. "We didn't touch anything. They carried it all into the house. And down the staircase into the basement," Bobby explains, his voice tinged with wonder and amusement. As they descended into the basement, they were greeted by yet another unexpected sight. "There's another replica, this one was of the set from The Mary Tyler Moore Show," he says, shaking his head in disbelief.

"It was complete with the six clocks on the wall. Quite elaborate and very close to what I remember from watching the show. We found out that Dark Shadows and The Mary Tyler Moore Show were his favorite two TV shows."

The basement was more than just a homage to television history, it was a fully equipped audio studio as well as a TV studio. "There was also a dressing room where attendants pressed their clothes and a buffet was laid out for them," Bobby said, still amazed at the setup.

The recording session began with The Embers performing "Far Away Places" and "I Love Beach Music." Bobby then stepped aside allowing Ammon Tharp to take the drums and lead on the Bill Deal and the Rhondells Medley, with The Embers featuring Craig Woolard providing backup. "It was quite an experience," Bobby mused. "We never actually saw Lubinsky." Despite the grandeur and meticulous planning, their host remained an elusive presence.

"*My Music: Summer, Surf & Beach Music We Love*," a presentation of T.J. Lubinsky's TJL Productions, premiered on PBS on August 22, 2016, with Mike Love of The Beach Boys serving as the emcee. Bobby notes, "The program showcased the contrasting and complementary styles of East Coast and West Coast beach music, making for an engaging and nostalgic viewing experience. A DVD and CD of the show was also released by Classic Masters.

Reflecting on the day, Bobby describes it as a whirlwind. "We left Raleigh about eight in the morning and got back about eleven at night." The experience was not just about the music but about the entire journey—the unexpected limousine ride, the stunning mansion replicas, and the professional yet surreal atmosphere in the basement studio. It was a day filled with surprises and memories that would last a lifetime.

CHAPTER 41

CHANGE CONTINUED its relentless rhythm. In August 2016, Gerald Davis returned to The Embers on bass, following Hugh Blanton's departure. Davis, formerly with The Embers for thirty-one years (1976-2007), brought a seasoned groove back to the ensemble.

On August 15, The Embers featuring Craig Woolard joined forces with The Impressions for a spectacular performance at Clinton, North Carolina, celebrating the 50th anniversary of the Williams Lake Dance Club. The year culminated with the North Carolina Public Television debut of the two-hour version of McBryde Films' documentary *"The Embers - The Heart and Soul of Beach Music"* on December 31, 2016, which continues to be rebroadcast in its entirety several times a year.

As summer turned to fall in 2017, it was shaping up to be another 250+ event-year for The Embers. Bobby Tomlinson had been the backbone of the band behind his drum kit for sixty years. However, his knee had been giving him problems off and on the last few years and had gotten progressively worse this year.

There were already twenty-eight dates on the December calendar. And these were The Embers' famous Christmas Shows. Lots of decorations, special sets, wardrobe changes, special musical instruments, and lots of logistics. Bobby was going to need some help this year to pull through it. And to top it all, the band had one of those "why-did-we-ever-agree-to-do-this" events staring them down in November. But it had a nice payday attached and Bogie and Bacall would dance to some Carolina Beach Music in Key Largo before they sailed away.

It was about eight hundred fifty miles from Raleigh to Key Largo, one way—fourteen hours of driving time. And the trip would be made over a two-day window as there were other events on the calendar on both sides of the Key Largo show. It would take two drivers to pull off the Key Largo round-tripper. So, Bobby called former bandmate Wayne Free, a solid horn blower, vocalist, and all-around Jack-of-all-trades. Wayne would join Bobby for the trip and split the driving responsibility.

Bobby usually drove the bus for events. Most of the trips were around the Carolinas, up to Virginia, and around Georgia so the driving wasn't too taxing. But with his knee bothering him more than usual, he decided to see his doctor before the South Florida trip.

The doctor took a quick look and ordered X-rays. The sixty years had taken their toll. It was now bone-on-bone. It wasn't just the top-hat cymbal pedal that was squeaking. His doctor advised him to prepare for knee replacement surgery and scheduled it for January 18, 2018. Bobby was relieved to have Wayne with them for the drive to and from Key Largo. Wayne was familiar with the Christmas Shows and all that was required of them.

And now, Bobby would need someone to fill in for him during his recovery over the winter.

The trip was indeed grueling. Bobby drove down to Miami where they rented a room for Wayne to get some much-needed rest, and the band went on to Key Largo for their performance. After the show concluded around 1 A.M., they drove back to Miami and picked up Wayne, who took the wheel and drove back to Raleigh. He was a lifesaver. Seeing Wayne's commitment and dedication, Bobby asked Wayne to join the team to get them through the holiday schedule. Wayne was playing with a Virginia band at the time, but he was able to work it out.

As the month progressed, Bobby began to discuss potential changes within the group as his surgery approached. Stephen Pachuta, who had been with The Embers for over a decade, primarily played trumpet but had some experience on drums.

One night driving back from a job, Bobby told Wayne, "I'm thinking about putting Stephen on drums. Maybe you'd like to come back and play trombone or trumpet?" Wayne, however, surprised Bobby by asserting "I play the drums better than Stephen."

Intrigued, Bobby arranged an audition for Wayne right after the New Year. The venue was the RDU Airport Sheraton on Interstate 40 on the night of January 6. The band assembled early, and Gerald Davis prepared three songs for Wayne to audition. Before the try-out, Bobby informed Craig Woolard that the final decision would rest with him and the other band members, as Bobby would be away for several weeks.

Wayne played the three songs, impressing the entire band. They all agreed he did a fantastic job. Craig, while initially uncertain if Wayne could manage the full load indefinitely, acknowledged his impressive performance. Everyone said they believed Wayne would be a good fit to get them through the uncertain period. Bob Blair, who had run sound for the Embers for years, had hours of tapes and videos that Free used to learn Bobby's drumming style and nuances that were Embers' trademarks.

Bobby informed Wayne that the fill-in spot was his. As was usually the case, The Embers had a light schedule for early January and would take a much-deserved two-week vacation. Reflecting on his age and the future of the band, Bobby made the decision not to return to his position. The January 6, 2018 show was his last. "Like I said, the rest is history, Bobby recalled. "I decided not to go back. At the time, I was nearing eighty years old. My thinking was that if I do go back, how much longer will I play? And if I let him go, we may not get anybody that good again, so I kept him, and he's been there ever since. He's doing a great job."

After six decades with the band, Tomlinson stepped away, marking the end of an era but ensuring the flame of The Embers would burn brightly into the future.

When asked if he missed it, Bobby smiled and remarked, "My arms start moving rapidly every night at about 8 o'clock."

Chapter 42

THE EMBERS HAVE LONG ENJOYED a special place in the hearts of music lovers in the Southeastern United States. But their influence extends far beyond the sandy shores of the Carolinas. Across the Atlantic, The Embers have become an integral part of the Northern Soul movement—a subculture born in the UK during the 1960s, focused on rare and obscure American soul records. A DJ spun an Embers record during a set at a UK nightclub in the 1970s, launching a unique transatlantic connection.

Northern Soul, with its roots in the 1960s mod scene, was a phenomenon that centered around the discovery of obscure American soul records with upbeat tempos perfect for dancing. Clubs like Wigan Casino and Blackpool Mecca became legendary venues where DJs would introduce rare tracks to packed dancefloors. The clubs featured "all-nighter" dance and record swap parties playing the rarest of US soul records with a freestyle dance reminiscent of US freestyle dancing. It was in these hallowed halls that several of The Embers' recordings took on new meaning.

Dr. Steve Baker, a dentist from Raleigh, North Carolina, first encountered The Embers in the 1960s as a teenager. Like many locals, he was drawn in by the sounds of Beach Music, a regional genre championed by radio DJ Charlie Brown on WKIX. Baker's love affair with The Embers began when he snuck into The Embers Club on Davie Street, despite being underage. From that moment, he was hooked.

"I listened to Charlie Brown on WKIX and he played many Embers' songs," Baker recalled. "When I got old enough to drive and be a little delinquent, I managed to sneak into The Embers Club, and I was hooked."

Baker's initial fascination with The Embers soon grew into an insatiable passion for collecting their records. Over the years, he has managed to acquire at least one of every piece of vinyl the band ever released. For Baker, the obsession was not just about the music but about possessing the tangible artifacts—the actual records.

"When you're a collector, you can't stand to have a song without having the actual record," he explained. "You've got to have the vinyl. Got to have it. Record collecting is the only addiction there's no cure for because there's always another one you don't have."

Beyond just collecting, Steve Baker became a critical figure in the Beach and Northern Soul communities. As a founding member of the Association of Beach and Shag Club DJs, Baker launched his Internet radio station, *Jukin' Oldies*. His weekly radio show, *The Northern Side of Soul*, highlights the intersection of his two greatest musical loves—Beach Music and Northern Soul. As the title suggests, Baker's show is the exemplification of how the musical legacies of the American South and the UK's

Northern Soul scene have intertwined, with The Embers serving as a key connector.

When asked to define "Northern Soul" and how The Embers fit into it, Baker explained: "Northern Soul is similar to Beach Music. It is a very broad term—a music and dance subculture developed in the UK in the 60s and 70s. It's like the blues—you've got slow country blues, and then you've got city blues. So, it's a big umbrella."

Another passionate collector who unearthed The Embers' contributions to the Northern Soul movement is John Peluso, a longtime record collector based in Raleigh-Durham, North Carolina. Originally from New Jersey, Peluso's fascination with local labels led him to a discovery that would introduce him to The Embers. "About twenty to twenty-five years ago, I would hear rumblings at the Raleigh Flea Market about JCP," Peluso shared. Intrigued, he asked, "What is JCP?" The answer sparked a journey that spanned decades and deepened his appreciation for the local Raleigh label that played a pivotal role in The Embers' early career.

Peluso found his first JCP 45 at an estate sale just a few houses down from his own. This discovery ignited a quest to collect all sixty-one 45s released on JCP, a label co-owned by Jimmy Capps, a popular local DJ, and Larry Gardner and Bill Hoke.

Peluso's meticulous work compiling the complete JCP discography revealed the rarity of The Embers' releases on the label, adding another layer of appreciation for collectors. "Most JCP releases averaged 500 pressings per title, but I believe The Embers releases might have been more due to their popularity," he speculated. This scarcity made The Embers' records particularly sought-after by Northern Soul collectors.

"I was a casual fan when I saw them perform at "Alive After 5" in downtown Raleigh on Thursday nights in the 1990s," he said. The bottom line is that they remain popular today, and that's not bad for a band that never hit the Top 100 on Billboard. I can still hear them today on AM 850 in Raleigh during Charlie Brown's weekly radio show "On The Beach" (now in syndication)."

E. Mark Windle, a UK-based freelance writer and collector, has long advocated The Embers' work. "It feels like the Northern Soul and Beach Music scenes have treasured The Embers' output forever," Windle remarked. One of the band's most cherished songs among collectors is "Far Away Places," which became a favorite in the Carolinas. But it was the B-side of that record, "Watch Out Girl," that captured the attention of Northern Soul fans. With its driving beat and emotional intensity, "Watch Out Girl" became a Northern Soul classic.

As Windle explained, the relationship between The Embers and the UK Soul scene deepened as collectors started unearthing more of the band's catalog. "The up-tempo "Where Did I Go Wrong" was first played in the early 1970s at Wolverhampton's Catacombs venue, way before Blackpool Mecca gave its stamp of approval," Windle noted. The legendary Wigan Casino, one of Northern Soul's most famous clubs, also embraced The Embers. By the early 1980s, DJs like Gary Rushbrook were spinning "Just Crazy 'Bout You Baby," adding the band to the register of Northern Soul greats.

Songs like "Watch Out Girl" captivated Northern Soul fans because of their undeniable danceability, paired with Jackie Gore's impassioned vocal delivery. The pounding backbeat, combined with sharp brass sections, created an irresistible call to the dancefloor, while the underlying emotional intensity of the lyrics struck a chord with listeners. "The thing about Northern Soul is that it's not just about rhythm—it's about the feeling behind the music," said Windle. "And The Embers had that in spades."

The Embers biggest chance for success came with their 1970 tune they recorded for MGM. The flip, "Watch Out Girl" is hot in English disco clubs.

Another key player in The Embers' Northern Soul story is Chris Beachley, owner of The Wax Museum Record Store in Charlotte, North Carolina, and founder of *It Will Stand,* a magazine dedicated to Beach Music. Beachley's store became a central hub for Beach Music fans. Over the years, it housed music of all genres and migrated to new formats as they emerged. "The Wax Museum wasn't just about sales, it was a place where stories were exchanged, friendships forged over

a mutual appreciation of these records," Beachley said. His magazine, *It Will Stand,* echoed this communal spirit. It covered The Embers frequently, through record and album reviews, and coverage of concerts and festivals where they appeared.

Beachley, a longtime supporter of The Embers, witnessed firsthand how their records became sought-after treasures for Northern Soul collectors, often fetching high prices due to their rarity. The Embers' early releases on the JCP label performed well in the Northern Soul market. "The early records, the ones they did on the JCP and eEe labels, command some decent prices as Northern Soul records," Beachley observed.

One of the most significant moments in Beachley's career was when he met with collectors from the UK who would travel to his Charlotte store to buy records in bulk. "Many of them came through my store and bought stuff," he noted. "And that really kind of affected the price, too."

In 2003, Beachley teamed up with WKIX icon Charlie Brown to produce *On The Beach*, a three-hour weekly radio show. Beachley wrote and produced the show, while Brown lent his inimitable voice and style as the host. The program continues today, syndicated on forty stations across six states, despite Brown's passing in 2022. "Of course, Charlie was big on The Embers," Beachley remarked.

Asked what he remembered most about the band, he said, "I heard Jackie Gore sing 'I Love Beach Music,' at a Charlotte club before they recorded it. And who can forget Jackie's Raymond Massey character? Raymond Massey was just such a cultural icon for the group, and people still talk about when he used to do that and how much they loved it. And, of course, Craig and his talents. He could sing Ray Charles one minute and Rod Stewart the next. I always thought that Jackie and or Craig could be national artists."

A new wave of recognition of The Embers' music overseas began to build in the 2020s. Mark Bicknell's Big

Man Records, a UK-based label specializing in rare soul reissues, released a remastered vinyl pressing of "Just Crazy 'Bout You Baby" and "Aware of Love," two songs that had long been favorites among Northern Soul collectors. The 2023 reissue, with historical liner notes penned by E. Mark Windle, marked yet another chapter in The Embers'

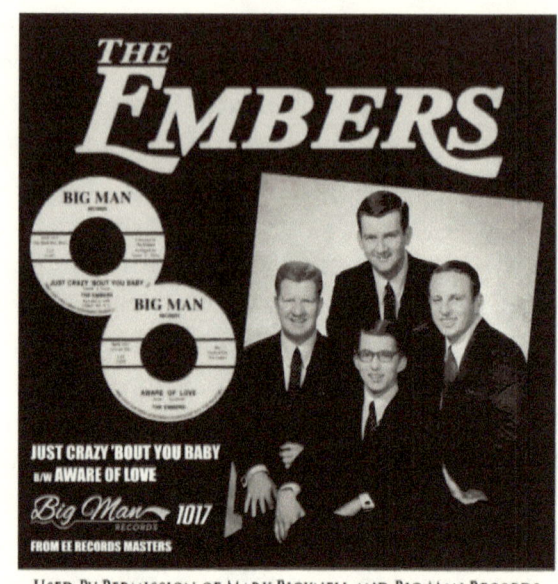

USED BY PERMISSION OF MARK BICKNELL AND BIG MAN RECORDS

Northern Soul legacy. Steve Baker's autographed 1966 Talent International Corporation promo picture of the band was featured in the liner notes, indicating how far-reaching and dedicated the fanbase has become.

The recent Big Man re-releases are great," observed JCP collector John Peluso. "How they mimicked the original label colors and fonts was just fantastic. The picture sleeves and liner notes were amazing. I hope they release more from The Embers catalog."

Their transatlantic appeal is proof that great music knows no borders—it simply finds a way to connect with those who are open to hearing it.

Epilogue

FOR OVER SIX DECADES, The Embers have held a unique place in Southern music and Northern Soul lore, particularly within the beach music community. Known for their memorable performances, infectious rhythms, and timeless melodies, The Embers became synonymous with good times and lasting memories along the Carolinas' coasts and beyond. As pioneers of a musical movement that continues to resonate with generations, their influence extends far beyond the dance floors and stages they once graced. And the band continues today.

At the heart of The Embers' legacy is Bobby Tomlinson, the band's original drummer and the driving force behind their success. From the band's inception in 1958, Bobby's steady hand and visionary leadership guided The Embers through lineup evolution and the ever-changing landscape of the music industry. His passion for innovation and commitment to excellence ensured that The Embers not only survived but thrived and remained a beloved institution in the world of beach music.

Julian Fowler, Beach Music Historian, sums it up this way, "They were professional. Every night their music was tight and it was a show. And when you left and walked out, you knew you'd seen something special that evening."

Mark Black put it this way, "I think The Embers set the standard. I think they set it a long time ago. I think they probably set it back in '67, '68 when they did 'Far Away Places.' I think that set the standard for beach music when the term 'beach music' came around. Then, of course, in '79 when they did 'I Love Beach Music,' that galvanized their place in beach music history."

Buzz Bolick said, "Being a club owner, in the twenty-five or thirty years I've used The Embers, that is the only band I've *never* lost money on. And that's pretty strong knowing all the great bands I've used. The Embers stand out way up above the others in all kinds of ways."

Paul Craver, Entertainment Director at Ducks Beach Club, credits The Embers as the group every band wanted to emulate. "When I first saw The Embers in the late 60s, when they hit the stage, all the girls ran to the stage and I said, 'I've got to do that. That's what I want to be.'

"They were such an inspiration to make me want to get into the music business. They were top-notch musicians and their format just dominated everything. Every other band copied The Embers or they didn't get much work.

"Seeing The Embers is a feeling that just grabs your body. It hit me at the age of eighteen in Greensboro at The Castaways, seeing The Embers, the music, the fun, the party, the dance, the buzz in the room. When The Embers stepped on the stage, they took it to another level."

John Hook, author and beach music historian, said, "There are a number of reasons why The Embers have endured the way they have. One, Bobby Tomlinson was a well-known dancer as a teenager. He won numerous dance contests and was able to transfer that rhythm to his drums. And two, he teamed up with Jackie Gore.

"In the world of beach music in the past fifty years, when I look at all the entertainers and all the performers and ask myself who in all of that has set a standard, I think of one person. And that's Jackie Gore."

JD Cash commented, "I just can't say enough about Jackie Gore. I mean, he's the best white male vocalist I've ever heard in my life—anywhere bar none. I mean, I've been all over. I've worked with Lou Rawls and James Brown. Nobody has that God-gifted voice like Jackie Gore. After I heard Jackie sing, it changed my whole direction. I stole a lot from him over the years. Trust me, we all did."

In this chronicle, we've had the privilege of hearing directly from Bobby Tomlinson himself—a man whose life and career are inextricably linked with The Embers. His reflections offer a deeply personal glimpse into the journey of a band that became a cultural icon, as well as the sacrifices and triumphs that marked their path. Through Bobby's eyes, we understand what it took to lead The Embers for more than sixty years, and the legacy he will leave behind.

Starting The Embers back in 1958 was just the beginning for him. "We didn't have a clear plan, but we had a passion for music and a drive to succeed. It wasn't easy, but we put in the work and over time we built something that lasted—something that still resonates with people today.

"We tried to stay out of politics. I always tried to adhere to Michael Jordan's advice of why he never ran for political office. He said that people of both political parties buy tennis shoes. Well, people of all political persuasions buy records.

"It was important to us that our music reached everyone, no matter their background or beliefs. We focused on what brought people together—the music.

"I'm just proud of the fact that I was able to start a band and be part of a band that started in 1958 and is still going strong. We created all that goodwill. That's what it was about for me—creating something good, something that made a positive impact. And it's humbling to see how that goodwill has endured through the years.

"There's not a week that goes by that I don't meet somebody who has something positive to say about the band. We played for their prom, we played for their wedding. They met their wife at The Embers Club. They did this, and they did that. And I'm proud of that.

"These connections, these memories, they're what made it all worth it. The Embers wasn't just a band, it was a part of people's lives, and that's something to cherish."

Donny Trexler, of Donny and Susan Trexler fame, told us about the time they hired The Embers to play at his birthday party at their home in Charlotte in 1982. "It rained all morning and we didn't have a place to put them if it didn't quit raining. And it quit raining about three o'clock in the afternoon and they were supposed to play at five.

"And here comes The Embers backing a tractor-trailer truck down my driveway. I was living in a new house and I was worried they were going to crack the driveway. But they backed this great big old truck down my driveway and unloaded the equipment. And I'd never seen so much equipment with a band in all my life. And I had a band called 'Swing' at the time that had a lot of equipment. But The Embers had a whale of a lot more equipment.

"They started playing at 5:30 and played until we finally went and told them the police came and told us we had to shut down. But we really had a good time. The Embers were great."

"This band was my life," Bobby said. "But it cost me three marriages. The Embers were everything to me, and I mean everything. It wasn't just a job—it was my obsession. The Embers came first in everything in my life. I was always thinking of what I could do to make it better. And I always wanted to be an innovator. I wanted to do something before anybody else could do it. Always thinking of the next big thing, always wanting to be first. And I think we did that. I mean, the greatest form of flattery is imitation.

"Being inducted into the Music Hall of Fame was a very special thing. That was a moment that validated all the hard work, all the sacrifices. But what I cherish most are the memories—opening the first Embers Club and the Embers Beach Club, and the others. Our times playing The Landmark and Coquina Club have to be up there. We were there for ten years. Those places weren't just venues, they were a part of who we were, a part of our story. "All those memories—they're what I'll hold onto forever."

ACKNOWLEDGEMENTS

As we bring "The Embers - The Bobby Tomlinson Story" to life, there are many people who deserve special recognition for their support, dedication, and contributions along the way.

First and foremost, we want to express our deepest gratitude to Bobby Tomlinson himself, the heartbeat of The Embers, for sharing his life, stories, and wisdom so generously. Bobby, your unwavering passion for music, your perseverance through decades of ups and downs, and your devotion to the legacy of beach music have been a constant source of inspiration. Thank you for allowing us the privilege of telling your story, and for your warmth, humor, and insights. This book would not exist without your trust and belief in this project.

To Bobby's nephew, John Tomlinson, Jr., thank you for your invaluable assistance in getting timely photos and information.

Others deserving recognition for sharing photos or information include Rickie Lipscomb, Jamie Reynolds and Johnny D. Johnson of Southeastern Camera, Cary Barneycastle, Gary Gibson, Bruce Blackman, Greg Haynes, Big John Ruth, and John Peluso.

Several former members of The Embers were instrumental in this project. Durwood Martin and Gerald Davis, we thank you for always being there to fill in a gap or details that were vital in this effort. Others who shared remembrances include Jackie Gore, Craig Woolard,

Johnny Hopkins, Frank Reich, John Thompson, Dave Norket, Johnny Barker, Blair Ellis, Mark Black, Buck Keener, and Wayne Free. It would not have been possible without you.

And special thanks to Keith Houston, JD Cash, Ralph Johnson, H. Lee Brown, Donny Trexler, Paul Craver, Charlie Brown, and Clifford Curry, who also provided valuable remembrances and information.

To Julian B. Fowler, thank you for sharing your knowledge, historical research, rare photos, and memorabilia. The background, information, and detailed discography you provided played an integral part in this project.

To John Hook, your valuable insights and observations gathered from your research on The Embers were extremely helpful.

To McBryde Films, whose 2014 documentary, *"The Embers - The Heart and Soul of Beach Music,"* was the inspiration and backbone of this book. The book draws on the documentary and the countless hours of interviews that Skip Crayton and Bill Benners conducted for their production which was almost five years in the making.

To the entire team at McBryde Publishing, thank you for your guidance, support, and expertise throughout this journey. Your commitment to preserving Carolina Beach Music's legacy through this book has been both motivating and invaluable.

We also want to extend our appreciation to the countless musicians, fans, and friends who have been part of Bobby's journey over the years. From the early days of The Embers to the grand stages of beach music festivals, this book reflects the community that made Bobby's career so remarkable.

Finally, to our families, your patience, encouragement, and belief in this project allowed us to dedicate the time and energy needed to bring Bobby's story to the world. We couldn't have done it without your unwavering support.

This book is not just a tribute to Bobby Tomlinson, it is a celebration of music, perseverance, and the enduring power of dreams. To everyone who played a part in this journey, we are deeply grateful.

Thank you.

ABOUT THE AUTHORS

CHRIS JONES, a retired public affairs executive, returned to his journalistic roots in 2022 after a 40-year corporate career working with government officials and regulatory leaders. A former radio deejay and news reporter, in 2023, Jones gained recognition for his article "White Fraternities and Black Music in the Early 60s," which explored the intersection of race and music during the formative years of Carolina Beach Music. The article, reprinted in a UK music magazine, received national attention and won a third-place award in feature writing from the National American Mature Publishers Association. "The Bobby Tomlinson Story" is his first book, marking a return to his passion for storytelling.

Jones resides near Athens, Georgia, with his wife, Toni, and remains active in local civic activities.

BILL BENNERS, owner of McBryde Publishing, is a best-selling author and seasoned storyteller with a career spanning over six decades in writing, publishing, and media production. His debut novel, *My Sister's Keeper*, became an international bestseller and has sold over a half-million copies. In addition to his success as a novelist, Benners has written and produced radio programs, editorials, and television content, as well as written for, directed, and acted in community theater.

He was also the co-author, director, and producer of the two-hour 2014 documentary film, *The Embers - The Heart and Soul of Beach Music*, a five-year endeavor with Skip Crayton, which airs periodically on North Carolina Public Television and is still available on DVD. A lifelong fan of The Embers, Benners brings his deep knowledge and passion to the writing of "The Bobby Tomlinson Story."

He resides in New Bern, North Carolina with his wife, Dorrie, their two beloved Morkies, and three totally demented cats.

SKIP CRAYTON is a writer, journalist, businessman, and community leader with a long history in North Carolina's literary and media landscape. Known for his insightful and engaging storytelling, Crayton has spent years documenting the culture and history of his beloved region. His first book, *Remember When* a collection of his newspaper columns about growing up in the 50s and 60s is a bestseller and in its 3rd printing. His second book, *The Letter Sweater*, a love story is also a bestseller with his third book *Life After Death*, a story of the trials of losing a loved one, is on its way.

His work with The Embers and their enduring legacy began over a decade ago when he first collaborated with Bill Benners on the documentary film *The Embers - The Heart and Soul of Beach Music*. With "The Bobby Tomlinson Story," Crayton brings his expertise in historical research and deep connections within the beach music world to the forefront, making this book a compelling tribute to a band that has defined a genre for over six decades.

Crayton resides in New Bern, North Carolina, with his wife Carol, and his two standard Poodles, Ruffin McNeil and New Bern Bear. And, oh yeah, those special times he and Carol get to spend with their grandson Crayton Dail.

TO CHRIS JONES

THIS JOURNEY to write a book about Bobby Tomlinson and The Embers began more than ten years ago with an agreement between Bobby Tomlinson, McBryde Publishing, Bill Benners, and Skip Crayton. Along the way that book got pushed aside when we (Bill and Skip) decided to make the PBS Documentary and hugely popular film, *The Embers - The Heart and Soul of Beach Music,* a priority. With almost five years of filming, interviewing, and traveling with the Embers, that film became a reality and a very successful one at that.

Yet, producing our original objective, the book, continued to simmer on the back burner. And simmer it did for too many years. But it just would not go away.

Enter Chris Jones.

It took a committed, seasoned writer with the same excitement that we had when we filmed those first scenes in Goldsboro, North Carolina, to rekindle that dream. We believe things happen exactly when they are supposed to and that God sends us what it takes to make dreams come true.

And that was Chris Jones.

Just a three-minute conversation with Chris about this project convinced us that he was the right person to partner with, in not only writing the story but with his extraordinary talent, to make the Bobby Tomlinson story of his life with The Embers a page-turning reality.

Chris, from two bestselling authors, our hats are off to you. You are that person who picked up the gauntlet and brought this story to life. It is you who made this book something we are both extremely proud to be a part of.

Skip Crayton and Bill Benners

MEMBERS OF THE EMBERS

Andy Swindell	1992-2001
Blair Ellis	1958-1962
Bobby Nance	2014-2022
Bobby Tomlinson	1958-2018
Buck Keener	1971-1976
Clay King	2007-2008
Craig Woolard	1976-2004, 2014-present
David Dixon	2007-2011
Dave Norket	1962-1964
Debbie Mack	2007-2008
Don Holloway	1969-1970
Don Jordan	1994-1995
Donnie Weaver	2004
Doug Harrison	1958-1961
Doug Strange	1976-1979
Durwood Martin	1964-1968, 1970-1976
Foy Biggers	1961-1963
Frank Reich	1963-1969
Fred Little	1969-1970
Freddy Tripp	2001-2003
Gerald Davis	1976-2007, 2016-present
Hugh "Tuff" Blanton	2013-2016
Jackie Gore	1958-1994
Jeff Grimes	1995-2007
Jeff Hayden	1994-1996
Jerry Tellier	2004-2008
Jimmy Weaver	2012-2013
John Ray	2008-2013

John Thompson	1968-1973, 1974-1976
Johnny Barker	1980-1990, 2004-2006
Johnny Hopkins	1967-2004
Jonathan Kuehling	2007
Josh Campbell	2007
Josh Shilling	2006-2007
Kevin White	2002-2004, 2023-present
Larry Haywood	1973-1974
Mark Black	1996-2004
Mark Hammer	1969-1970
Matt Kosma	2009-2011
Randy Hignite	1990-1991
Ray Brooks	1970-1971
Ray Rivera	1969-1970
Rick Whitfield	1968-1969
Ricky Sanders	2008-2012
Russell Carter	1962-1963
Stephen Pachuta	2006-2023
Waylon Jones	1968
Wayne Free	2004-2014, 2017-present

Bobby's Honorable Mentions:

Janice "Peaches" Sinquefield (Fill-in Vocalist) 1962
Willie McDougal (Fill-in Keyboardist)   1960s

EMBERS' CREW & SPECIALIST MEMBERS

Mike Morgan	1971-1978	Sound
Freddy Tripp	1974	Truck Driver/Roadie
Gaylon Pope	1978-1979	Bus Driver
David Emory	1978-1980	Sound
Steve Foley	1979-1980	Lights
Randy McKeel	1980	Crew
Bob Wilmuth	1980	Sound
Graham Wiggs	1980	Sound
Joe Yanulevich	1980	Lights
Jeff Hines	1980-1981	Crew/Lights
Steve Davis	1980-2007	Sound
Jay Rogers	1981-1988	Lights
B.B. Nation	1981-1986	Crew
Robin Kirth	1982-1984	Crew/Monitors
Tommy Albert	1982-1984	Crew/Lights
Weasel Young	1983-2007	Stage Monitors
Kelly Allen	1984-1986	Stage Monitors
David Haskell	1984-1988	State Monitors
Eb Strickland	1984-1987	Stage Monitors
Keith Eubanks	1997-2024	Truck Driver/ Stage Monitors/ Lights
Mark Nordan	1987	Crew
Matt Naylor	1988-1995	Sound
Randy Webster	1994-1995	Crew
Bill Lochhart	1995-1996	Crew
John Swett	1995-1997	Truck Driver
Tommy Nichols	1997	Truck Driver
Mike Camp	1998-1999	Sound

Gene Youngblood	2000	Truck Driver
Terry Garrett	2000-2002	Sound
Dee Shankle	2001-2003	Stage Monitors
Bill Safrit	2004-2008	Sound
Kevin Wright		Sound
Bryan Hitzigrath		Sound
Dustin Bradley		Sound
Rob Heller		Monitors
John Bonner		Monitors
Pat Kendall		Lights
Mike Sabato		Truck Driver
Jimmy Batts		Truck Driver
Chopper Kovich	2016	Sound
Kelly Mon	2016	Stage Monitors
Bob Blair	2016-2024	Sound
Ben Brown	2019-Present	Merchandise

EMBERS' BLUEWATER INVESTORS

Dr. William A. Ballance, Jr.
Larry Tysinger
Jim Abbott
Joseph Cato
Thomas E. Cato
Waylon Cato III
Curtis L. Edmondson
John D. and Sandy Judy
William Randolph and Renee Jones
Noel Hankin
William P. Hinson III
Mack L. and Carol Barnhill
JoAnn M. Smith
Dona I. Hill

EMBERS' SPONSORS

AKG Microphones
Budweiser   Bob Fuller, Jim Zink, Jim
                                 Yates, Bobby Pecht
Freightliner Trucks   Larry Tysinger
Pepsi   Jeff Minges, Tom Barnes
Alexander Julian   Alex Julian
Ruff Hewn   Jeff H. Rives
Capezio Shoes   Kevin Smith
Heritage Bank   John Tilton
NC Tourism Department   Gordon Clapp, Dick Tramell,
                                 David Little
Dillard's   Ron Garland
Piggly Wiggly   Bill McLeod, Buzzy Newton III
Hayes Jewelry   Bruce Hayes
Jams World   David Poe Rochlen

SPECIAL RECOGNITION

We extend our deepest gratitude and sincere appreciation to Dr. William A. Ballance, Jr., whose unwavering support and generosity have guided The Embers through many years. His vision, availability, willingness to help, sound advice, counsel, and innovative ideas have been instrumental to the band's success. We are forever grateful for his dedication and steadfast belief in The Embers.

Bobby Tomlinson & The Embers

INDEX

10th Avenue 174
1981 Beach Music Medley 146
25th Anniversary 165
39-21-46 .... 114, 119
42nd Street. 201
60-Minute Man .. 102, 105, 113, 169
A Touch of Gentleness 24
A White Sport Coat 21
Ace Records 32, 33, 48
Achy Breaky Heart 165
Across The Street 119
Ain't No Big Thing . 66, 67, 119
Air Force 25
Alabama 32
Alabama Theatre's Christmas Show 210
Alexander Julian 154
All My Lovin 48
Always In Love 144
AM 850 231
American Ambassador 196
American Idol 200
Americana Garden Apartments 100, 102
Ammon Tharp 189, 220, 221, 222
Andre the Giant 109
Andy Griffith 192
Andy Swindell 165, 166, 179, 217, 218, 251
Anheuser-Busch 123, 124, 136, 138
Animal Crackers 139
Annual DJ Throwdown 198
Appalachian State 176
Archie Bell and The Drells 59, 73, 74, 81, 85
Arthur Murray Dance Studio 110
Arthur Smith Studio .. 63, 124, 146
Arthur Wilson 192
Asheboro 162
Association of Beach and Shag Club DJs 229
Association of Beach and Shag DJ's 198
Association of Carolina Shag Clubs 133
Astors 32
At the Buckhead Beach 139, 140, 141
At The Sands Hotel Resort and Casino .. 187
Atco label 10
Atlanta 86, 87, 116

Atlanta Beach Music Festival 133
Atlanta Showcase . 89, 100
Atlantic Beach .. 38, 68, 69, 72, 73, 74, 81, 86, 192
Atlantic City 184, 187
Atlantic label 10
Atlantic Ocean 122
Atlantic Records 65, 174
Aubrey Mason 69, 74
August Busch 124, 125, 126
Ava Gardner 192
Aware of Love 66, 234
B.B. King 20
B.J. Thomas 73, 108
Baby What You Want Me To Do 174
Bailey, North Carolina 109
Band of Oz 73, 135, 153, 165, 173, 197
Barbara Lewis 66
Barber Communication 151
Barnie Pip 44
Beach Beat 65
Beach Boys 50, 51, 52
Beach Music .. 77, 200, 201, 229
Beach Music Awards . 199
Beach Music Encyclopedia 109
Beach Music Workout 180, 181
Beatles 45, 47, 48, 49
Beautiful Things 109

Bee Gees 132
Beethoven's Fifth 120
Before Six 54
Begin The Beguine Medley 183
Bell Records 65, 67
Ben E. King 174
Bert Caudle ... 61, 62, 66, 67
Besamé Mucho 204
Best Classic Song 199
Best Club Song 199
Better Brands 123
Big Bopper 93
Big Jack Armstrong 44
Big John Band 207
Big John Ruth 241
Big Man Records 234
Bill "Puss" Jenkins 83
Bill Ballance . 208, 217, 259
Bill Benners 4, 119, 167, 242
Bill Clinton 176
Bill Deal and the Rhondells ... 189, 220, 222
Bill Duncan 23
Bill Griffin 108
Bill Hoke 230
Bill Lowery 140, 184
Bill Monroe 18, 20
Bill Pinkney 178
Bill Pinkney's Drifters 107, 122
Bill's Barbecue 195
Billboard Magazine 52, 142
Billy Ray Cyrus 165
Bing Crosby 74

262

Black Jack Daniels 78
Black music .. 10, 33, 34, 66
Black musicians 34
Black sax player 27, 28, 31
Blackjack Mulligan 109
Blackpool Mecca. 228, 231
Blair Ellis 22, 23, 25, 30, 35, 38, 242, 251
Blood, Sweat & Tears .. 86
Blue Decorations 151
Blue Moon 35
Blue Tower Restaurant 58
Bluegrass Band 18
Blues Brothers 153
Bluewater Records 199, 205, 207
Bob Blair 227
Bob Collins and The Fabulous Five 73
Bob Fuller 124
Bob Hope....................... 186
Bob Jones 46
Bob Kelly 47
Bobby Bland 28
Bobby Davis 145
Bobby Nance 217, 251
Bobby Pecht 151
Bobby Purify 160
Bobby Tomlinson 251
Boca Raton 127
Bogie and Bacall......... 225
Brenda 199
Bring It On Home to Me 178
British 45
Broadway 201

Broughton High School Marching 100 16
Bruce Blackman 180, 181, 241
Buck Keener.... 87, 93, 100, 101, 103, 104, 242, 251
Buckhead Beach 133, 139, 141, 165
Buddy Hawkins 119
Buddy Holly 20
Buddy Skipper 32, 38
Budweiser.... 122, 123, 124, 127, 136, 149, 151, 257
Burl Ives 211
Burn You A New One . 60, 66, 67
Buzz Bolick.............. 95, 236
Cal Duke 184
California 61
Call Me.......................... 207
Cameron Village.......... 192
CAMMY Awards . 171, 176, 178, 182
Canada 89
Canadian....................... 158
Canadian Prime Minister Jean Chrétien 196
Canadian Sunset 144, 179, 180, 182, 183
Candy 32
Cape Fear River 162
Carl Wilson..................... 52
Carlen Records............. 183
Carolina Beach............. 192
Carolina Beach Music.. 3, 4, 121, 177

263

Carolina Beach Music Awards 120, 171, 176, 182, 197
Carolina Beach Music Encyclopedia 76
Carolina Beach Music Hall of Fame 120
Carter-Finley Stadium 153
Cary Barneycastle 241
CBMA 197
Center Court Lounge 100, 102, 108
Chairmen of the Board 122, 135, 220
Chantilly Lace 93
Chapel Hill 139
Charles Wallert ... 198, 199, 200, 202, 207
Charlie Barksdale 184, 189, 197
Charlie Brown ... 46, 47, 49, 50, 65, 66, 67, 92, 229, 231, 233, 242
Charlie Daniels Band 154
Charlie's Place 66
Charlotte 42, 63, 115
Charlotte's Mangold-Bertos 75
Cheaters Never Win .. 118, 159
Chester Mayfield and the Casuals 59
Chicago 44, 86
Chris Beachley 76, 115, 119, 232, 233
Chris Biehler 198

Christmas Memories .. 150
Christmas Show 211
Christmas with The Embers 205, 208
Chuck Berry 20, 75
Cincinnati Conservatory of Music 23, 25
Clarence "Frogman" Henry 35
Clarence Carter 85
Classic Master 223
Clay Aiken 219
Clay King 207, 208, 251
Clemson University 148
Cleveland 44
Cliff Ellis 148
Clifford Curry 242
Clyde Moody 17, 18
Coca-Cola 178
Coca-Cola Classic 178
Colours 154, 158
Columbia 42, 62, 103
Cool Me Out 147
Coors Silver Bullet Band 152
Cooter Ridge Armadillo Hunt Club 157
Coquina Club .. 97, 98, 130, 239
Cornelius Brothers and Sister Rose 108, 112, 122
Cortez Greer 85, 91, 107, 108
Count Basie 20
Cousin Brucie 44
Cowboys to Girls 155

Craig Woolard... 68, 91, 92, 93, 96, 103, 105, 109, 134, 143, 144, 145, 147, 154, 166, 168, 198, 200, 217, 219, 233, 241, 251
Craig Woolard Band . 217, 218
Creators: Artists and Inventors Whose Work Shape Our State and The Nation's Perception 192
Cruisin' 200
Cuba Gooding 199
Curtis Mayfield 54, 93
Dan Duryea 51
Dave Clark Five 46
Dave Norket 38, 39, 242, 251
David Dixon . 207, 219, 251
David Little 161
Davie Street 57, 81, 229
Dean Martin 186
Debbie Dobbins 178
Debbie Mack 207, 208, 251
Deeper in Love 154
Del Rio, Texas 44
Dennis Wilson 52
Dewey Brothers Foundry 6
Diana Ross 132
Dick Allen 75
Dick Clark's Caravan of Stars 35
Dick Duryea 51, 52
Dick Trammel 161

Did You Boogie With Your Baby 173, 179
Dink Perry's Breeze Band 217
Dionne Warwick 66, 78
Division of Tourism, Film, and Sports Development 191
Dixie 52
Doc Watson 192
Documentary film ... 4, 26, 119, 120, 166, 218, 224, 242
Dodger baseball game 126
Don Holloway 251
Don Jordan . 173, 174, 175, 251
Don Perry 98
Don Ross 129, 149
Don't Feel Rained On 174
Donald King 24
Donald King and The Juniors 23
Donna Summer 132
Donnie Weaver ... 202, 208, 251
Donny and Susan Trexler 238
Donny Trexler 117, 238, 242
Dorton Arena 50
Dot Com Your Ass 183
Doug Clark and the Hot Nuts 31, 73
Doug Clark and The Hot Nuts 32

Doug Harrison .. 27, 28, 38, 251
Doug McKendrick 139, 140
Doug Strange 104, 251
Drowning in the Sea of Love 166
Ducks Beach Club...... 236
Dudley, NC........................ 9
Duke Ellington................ 20
Duke Hall 151
Duke University 196
Dunhill Compact Classics 151
Durham..................... 13, 32
Durwood Martin...... 38, 39, 42, 53, 54, 76, 93, 100, 101, 103, 104, 202, 219, 241, 251
Dusty Rhodes................ 109
E. Mark Windle... 231, 232, 234
Earl Dawkins................. 165
Earl Dawkins' Entertainers.............. 217
eEe label 233
El Paso............................. 93
Elliot Murnick................ 65
Elton John 93, 109
Elvis Presley 20
Ember Records 26
Ember's 25th Anniversary............... 141
Embers Beach Club 72, 73
Embers Beach Medley 143
Embers Beach Music Medley 81 138
Embers Booking Agency 63
Embers Club 59, 60, 68, 72, 81, 83, 84, 85, 91, 129
Embers Club Hilton Underground 109
Embers Entertainment Enterprises.......... 62, 179
Embers Hilton Underground 108
Embers Live in Center Court Lounge 181
Embers Live—A Landmark Experience 179
Embers Records 166
Embers Roll Eleven 47
Embers' Beach Medley '81 143
Emerald Isle Beach Music Festival 122
English 46
Entertainer of the Year 199
Erdahl Cloyd Union 48
Esso Station 39
Eveready Man 166
Eye of The Tiger........... 131
Far Away Places 76, 81, 83, 146, 179, 180, 203, 222, 231, 236
Fat Harold's Beach Club 133, 167
Fats Domino 20, 35, 85
Fayetteville 98
Feel The Heat 163, 166
Female vocalist 36

Finger Poppi Time 184
Fingers Taylor 177
Fire Marshal 82
First Annual Beach
  Music Awards Show
  144
Florida 92
Fool in Love 55
Fool In Love 119
Fools Rush In 166
Forevermore Records 198
Fort Wayne 44
Foy Biggers 38, 251
Frank Reich. 38, 53, 63, 69,
  73, 79, 242, 251
Frank Sinatra 87, 186
fraternity 31
Fred Little 87, 251
Freddy Tripp 197, 198, 199,
  251
Freightliner 156
Friday Night 178
Full Sail 101
Full Sail Productions. 148
Gary Gibson 241
Gary Rushbrook 231
Gene and Ole Anderson
  109
Gene Barber and the
  Cavaliers, ... 74
Gene Fowler and the
  Falcons 21, 23
Gene Jones 22, 25
General Aycock ... 213, 215
George Bailey 23
George Benson 199
Georgia Tech 142

Gerald Davis 103, 104, 114,
  118, 126, 127, 134, 136,
  143, 145, 169, 179, 182,
  187, 189, 203, 206, 224,
  226, 241
Get Ready 53, 66
Girl (Why You Wanna
  Make Me Blue 53
Gold Park Lake 9
Golden Years 117
Goldsboro 6, 7, 9, 11, 12, 41,
  104
Goldsboro High School
  Marching Earthquakes
  .... 7, 8, 9
Good Good Lovin' 50
Gordon Clapp 163
Gordon Giffin 196
Governor James B. Hunt
  195
Grand Ole Opry 18
Grand Strand 97
Grant Lewis 155, 156
Green Eyes 102
Green's Studio 32
Greensboro 108, 117
Greg Haynes 241
Gross Records 32
Group of the Year 199
Group Vocalist of the
  Year 199
Gypsy Woman 48
H. Lee Brown 167, 242
Hang On Sloopy 52
Hank Williams 20
Having A Party 119
Having My Baby 93

Hawaii 127
He Will Break Your
    Heart 119
Help Me Rhonda 50
Heritage Golf
    Tournament 148
Hey Baby 119, 207
Hillsborough Street 49
Hilton 108
Hilton Head 148
Hilton Hotels 106
Hilton Underground
    Embers Club 113
Hilton Underground
    Embers Club, ... 108
Hip Pocket 101
Hit Attractions Agency 63, 78
Holiday Inn 52
Holiday Inn Travel Park
    122
Holly Jolly Christmas 211
Homer Briarhopper 17, 18
Hook, Line, and Sinker
    204
Hot Nuts, Get 'Em From
    The Peanut Man 33
How Sweet It Is 119
Hugh "Tuff" Blanton . 217, 224, 251
Hugh Morson Junior
    High School 11, 15
Hugh Rodgers 87, 89
Hugh Rodgers Agency 87, 100
Hurt So Bad 60

I Got You (I Feel Good)
    145
I Love Beach Music ... 114, 115, 116, 118, 119, 120, 128, 165, 179, 180, 186, 192, 222, 233
I Love Budweiser 122, 124, 125, 138
I Love My Baby 24
I Wanna Be (Your
    Everything) 166
I'm A Girl Watcher 108
I'm Gonna Do Beautiful
    Things For You 108, 118, 179
I'm On The Outside
    Looking In 54
I'm So Lonely 33
I'm Your Puppet 160
I've Been Hurt 207
I've Done Things With
    You 208
In My Lonely Room 50
In the Still of the Night 26
Interagency Tourism
    Fair. 194
Interfraternity Council 52
Ira David Wood 154
Irresistible You 54
It Ain't Necessary 65, 67
It Ain't the Meat (It's the
    Motion) 204
It Will Stand 114
It Will Stand Magazine
    .... 76, 232
It Will Stand Magazine.
    119

J. William (Bill) Harvey 155
J.C. Meyers 161
J.D. Cash 74
Jack Brinkley 156
Jack Sullivan 21, 22
Jackie .39, 40, 42, 58, 60, 91, 93, 94, 99, 100, 103, 110, 120, 122, 127, 130
Jackie Gore . 11, 12, 13, 21, 33, 71, 74, 77, 79, 81, 103, 104, 109, 113, 115, 120, 121, 134, 144, 154, 166, 179, 180, 231, 233, 237, 241, 251
Jackie Hamilton 33
Jackie Wilson 59, 74, 78, 85
Jackie Wilson Medley 156
Jacksonville 39
James Brown 10, 28, 50, 63, 64, 75, 87, 144, 145
James Brown Live at the Apollo 144
Jamie Reynolds 241
Jams World 186, 187
Jan and Dean 220
Jane Fonda 179, 180
Janice "Peaches" Sinquefield 252
Janice Sinquefield .. 36, 37
Janis Joplin 86
Jay Spell 178
JCP 50, 65
JCP Records 49, 53, 230, 233
JCP Studios 207
JD Cash 237, 242

Jeb Bush 189
Jeff Grimes .. 174, 175, 179, 183, 202, 206, 216, 217, 251
Jeff Hayden .. 173, 179, 251
Jeff Hires 154
Jekyll Island Beach Music Festival 133
Jerry Butler 66, 78, 177
Jerry Goodman 75
Jerry Lee Lewis 35
Jerry Polk 202
Jerry Tellier . 201, 206, 208, 251
Jerry Wexler 65, 66
Jesup, Georgia 154
Jetty Jumpers 32, 38
Jillian Rand 57
Jim Crockett 50, 51
Jim Crow era 31
Jim Lewis 55
Jim Mieler 106
Jim Thornton 37, 58, 59
Jim Thornton's Dance Club 34, 35, 37, 57
Jim Thornton's Saturday Night Country Style . 33
Jimi Hendrix 89
Jimmy Capps 47, 48, 49, 50, 62, 230
Jimmy Florence 21, 22
Jimmy Hall 177
Jimmy Weaver 216, 251
Jingle Bells 211
Joe Boylan 147
Joe Cocker 109
Joe Murnick . 50, 51, 54, 65

Joe Pope Pioneer Award 197
Joe Saraceno 75
John B. Thompson 7, 8, 9, 41
John Coltrane 192
John Dockery................152
John Ellison 178
John Hook.......76, 101, 109, 119, 144, 145, 202, 237, 242
John O.D. Williams.......83
John Peluso..230, 234, 241
John R..........................10, 44
John Ray 208, 219, 251
John Thompson 76, 79, 92, 93, 100, 101, 103, 104, 105, 167, 242, 252
John Tomlinson, Jr.....241
Johnny Adams..............178
Johnny Barker.......90, 116, 134, 144, 145, 202, 208, 242, 252
Johnny Cash 20
Johnny D. Johnson ...241
Johnny Hopkins......77, 92, 95, 100, 103, 104, 127, 134, 145, 167, 168, 242, 252
Jonathan Kuehling....207, 252
Josephus Daniels High School.............................15
Josh Campbell.....207, 252
Josh Shilling..........206, 252
Jukin' Oldies 229
Julian Fowler 48, 116, 236, 242

Junior Walker 93
Junior Walker and The All Stars, ...73
Just Crazy 'Bout You Baby 231, 234
Just For The Birds .53, 54
Kappa Sig 28, 31
Kappa Sigma 28
Keith Houston........73, 179, 207, 242
Kelly McCoy 119
Ken Barnes 22, 23, 25
Ken Knox 220
Ken Pierce, ...23
Kevin White...199, 202, 252
KHP Music 179
KHP Records.................207
King David & The Slaves 156
King's Plaza....................129
King's Plaza Embers Club.............................129
KISS..................................109
Kitty Hawk 200
Korea........................208, 213
Lake Pontchartrain 89
Lake Wheeler................112
Landmark Resort Hotel 97, 108, 123, 129, 134, 138, 146, 149, 239
Larry Gardner 47, 230
Larry Haywood........91, 252
LaRue.....................113, 166
Las Vegas...................61, 87
Lavern Baker 37

Lawrenceville, VA, Live Beach Music Festival 151
Led Zeppelin 132
Lee Dorsey 174
Les Paul guitar 27
Let It Snow, Let It Snow, Let It Snow 211
Let's Have a Party 177, 182
Linda 36
Linda Griffith 36
Ling Ting Tong' 10
Link Wray 219
Little Anthony 85
Little Anthony and the Imperials 60
Little Darling I Need You 119
Little Esther Phillips .. 174
Little Eva Boyd 219
Little Honda 50
Little Hugh and The Embers 87
Little Mama 204
Little Richard 13, 20, 28, 75
Little Young Lover 54
Live at the Sands 196
Liverpool 45
Livin' For The Weekend 178
Livin' It Up 178
Locomotion 219
Lonely Teardrops 156
Lou Rawls 124
Louis Armstrong 20, 28, 87

Love Don't Come No Stronger 198
Love Falling 166
Love Me 144
Love Potion Number Nine 36
Lovey Dovey 204
Lowe's hardware store 17
Lowe's North Wilkesboro Hardware 18
Lubinsky 222
Maceo Parker 177
Male Vocalist of the Year 199
Manteo 162
Marion Carter 118, 178, 182
Mark Bicknell 233
Mark Black 77, 167, 176, 179, 198, 201, 202, 236, 242, 252
Mark Hammer 252
Mark McGregor 155
Marriott 150
Marsha Hancock 199
Marshall Sehorn 32
Martha Reeves & The Vandellas 50
Marty Robbins 21, 93
Marvin Gaye 42, 48
Master Sound Studio 140
Matt Kosma .. 208, 219, 252
Maurice Williams and the Zodiacs 59, 108
May I 207
Maynard (Cutie) Mosley 70

MCA 75
McBryde Films 120, 218, 224, 242
McBryde Publishing ... 242
Mega Sound Studio 109
Mel Strickland 21, 23
Memorial Auditorium .. 78
Memphis 20
Memphis Soul 177
Men of Music 47, 50, 65
Metro Club 103
Mexican Divorce 65
MGM Records 75, 76, 81, 83
Miami 89
Michael and Tony . 92, 100
Michael and Tony Designs 89
Michael Braun 89, 91
Michael Jackson 132
Michael Reineri 47, 48
Mick Jaggar 54
Mickey and Sylvia 107
Mike Curb 75, 76
Mike Gordon 75
Mississippi Gulf Coast 180
Moms Mabley 87
Money, Money, Money. 24
Moonglow 183
Moonlight Feels Right 181
Motown 42, 52, 177
Ms. Grace 119
Ms. Grace, ... 113
Muddy Waters 20
Murphy 162
Music Hall of Fame 239

Musical Ambassadors of Good Will 191, 194
My Baby 53
My Girl 52
My Girl Sloopy 53
My Music: Summer, Surf & Beach Music We Love 222
Myrtle Beach 66, 95, 97, 99, 129, 133, 153
Myrtle Beach Convention Center. 144, 154
Nashville 44
Nashville, Tennessee 10
National Anthem 148
NC State .. 25, 28, 31, 38, 47, 49, 53, 70, 148, 184
NC State Fairgrounds .. 51
Needham Broughton High School 15
Neil Young 192
Never Give Up 208
New Bern 28, 39, 71
New Century Platters ... 97
New Orleans 20, 44, 89, 124
New York 61
New York City 44
News and Observer 55, 82, 83, 191
Nick Hice 146, 151
Nigel Olsen 109
North Carolina Department of Tourism, Film, and Sports Development 194

272

North Carolina Music Hall of Fame............. 219
North Carolina Public Television................... 224
North Carolina Style. 163, 166
North Carolina Tourism and Economic Development............ 195
North Carolina's Ambassadors of Tourism...................... 200
North Carolina's Musical Ambassadors of Goodwill..................... 163
North Myrtle Beach .. 129, 151
North Wilkesboro, North Carolina....................... 17
Northern Soul..... 228, 229, 230, 231, 233, 234
Novas IX 217
Nuts To You 32
O.C. Smith..................... 199
Ocean Beach................ 192
Ocean Drive '95 sampler 173
Ocean Drive South..... 133
Olympics 151
On The Beach...... 231, 233
On The Rocks 208
Oo Poo Pah Doo 207
Ooh Poo Pah Doo 55
Oriole Stadium............. 150
Orlando.................. 89, 100
Ottawa, ... 195
Palm Beach 89

Panthers game 190
Papa's Got a Brand New Bag................................. 65
Paramount Theatre........ 7
Party Time Man........... 178
Patti LaBelle and the Bluebelles 54, 55
Paul Anka 93
Paul Craver... 108, 236, 242
Pavilion 38, 68, 69, 70, 74
PBS 222
Peace College 31
Peaches..................... 36, 37
Peachtree 139
Peachtree Street............ 89
Pepsi 202, 257
Perry Como..................... 74
Phil Upchurch Comb... 28
Philip Littleton............... 10
Phoenix, Arizona........... 37
Piedmont Airlines....... 195
Piggly Wiggly 178, 205
Piggly Wiggly Presents The Embers 205
Pink Floyd..................... 132
Pittsburgh....................... 87
Polo's Lounge & Embers Beach Club151, 152, 153
Porter Wagoner 18
President George H.W. Bush........................... 189
President George W. Bush................... 189, 200
Pres-Jax................. 208, 216
Pres-Jax Records........ 208
Preston's Seafood Restaurant................ 153

Pretty Paul Jones 109
Public Broadcasting
  Service 220
Puerto Rico 28
R&B 44, 48, 54, 65, 78
Radio stations 44
Raleigh 11, 12, 24, 32, 39,
  45, 54, 61, 65, 108
Raleigh Flea Market ... 230
Ralph Johnson 97, 99, 242
Randy Gore 21, 22
Randy Hignite 165, 252
Randy Watson 184, 188,
  189, 196, 198
Rare Beach Sounds 76
Ray Brooks 252
Ray Charles 20, 38, 93, 146, 233
Ray Rivera 77, 252
Raymond Massey . 93, 130, 233
Ready To Roll 166
Red's Beach Music Club
  183
Reece Culbreath 151
Reflection Studio 116
Reno 87
Reputation 60
Reynold's Coliseum 54, 109
Rhythm & Blues 52
Rhythm & Blues
  Network 200
Rhythm and Blues 10, 12,
  34, 47, 144, 159, 192
Richard DuPree 21
Richard Simmons 179, 180

Rick Dees 47
Rick Flair 109
Rick Sanders 219
Rick Simmons 76
Rick Whitfield 252
Rickie Lipscomb 241
Ricky Sanders 208, 252
Ricky Steamboat 109
Riddick Stadium 53
Ripete 151, 184
Ripete Records 118, 165,
  166, 177, 178, 182, 200
Rob Barber 147, 151
Robert Ray 140
Robert Trammell 159
Roberta Flack 153
Rock and Roll Heaven . 93
Rock 'n' Roll 20
Rockin' Around the
  Christmas Tree 211
Rockin' Crickets 54
Rocking Pneumonia ... 119
Rod Stewart 233
Roger Wise 10
Romeo Davis 75
Rose Beth label, ... 24
Ruff Hewn 154, 257
Rufus Thomas 59
Russell Carter 252
S.O.S.. ..... 166, 183, 200, 201
Sam and Dave 78
Sam Cooke 20
Sam Zabowski 150
Sammy Davis Jr 186
San Diego 127
Sands Casino 185, 186

Sands Hotel and Casino 184
Santa Claus Is Coming To Town 151
Saturday Night Fever 201
Savannah 89
Scarlett O'Hara's 86
Searchin' 48
Sears Roebuck and Company 61
Second Chance Band 155, 156
Secret Service 189
September in the Rain 182
Shag 133
Shake a Tail Feather . 160
Sharon (Henshaw) Copeland 36
Shay McNeal 139
Shimmying in a Winter Wonderland 33
Sigma Nu 155
Simon Dixon 23
Since I Lost My Baby .. 53
Sister Sledge 174
Skip Crayton ... 4, 119, 120, 167, 242
Smith-McNeal Advertising Agency. 139
Smoke Gets in Your Eyes 155
Smokey Joe's Café 201
Smokey Robinson 200
So Rare 182
Society of Stranders, also see S.O.S 166

Someday 174
Sonny & Cher 78
Sonny Turner and Sound Limited 85
Sonny Turner' Platters 108
South Carolina Beach Music Hall of Fame 219
South Carolina R&B/Beach Music Hall of Fame 197
South Carolina Rhythm and Blues Hall of Fame 219
Southbound Train 173
Southeastern Camera 241
Sports Music, Inc. 180
Spring Safari 183
Spud Spadoni 123
St. Louis 124
St. Petersburg 89
Starbuck 181
Stars on 45 .... 118, 182
Statesville 95
Statesville Country Club 116
Stephen Pachuta 205, 206, 219, 226, 252
Steve Baker 229, 234
Steve Leonard 150
Steve Owens and Summertime 216
Steve Roddy 46
Stevie Wonder 132
Stik McGhee 65
Street Corner Serenade 178

String of Pearls 183
Stubborn Kind of Fellow
 .... 48, 52, 55
Studio East 151
Summertime's Calling
 Me 114
Surf 94.9 FM 120
T.J. Lubinsky 220, 222
Take Care of You For Me
 144
Talent International
 Associates..................... 62
Talent International
 Corporation................ 234
Talent Residuals........... 126
Tallahassee 159
Tampa................................ 86
Tampa Bay 89
Tar Heel State 191
Teasing You 66
Ted Hall...................... 63, 78
Tennessee Waltz............. 18
Teresa Brewer 37
Terri Evans 139
Terri Gore 166
Terry Garrett 195
Texas.................................. 89
TGIF 178
The Avengers................. 165
The Beach Boys ... 180, 220
The Bell Airs 37
The Blues Other
 Brothers...................... 153
The Boondocks 117
The Breeze Band 197
The Carolina Beach
 Music Hall of Fame 176

The Castaways 74, 108,
 122, 216
The Castaways Combo 36
The Catalinas 59, 108, 116,
 135, 152, 173, 217
The Chosen Few 154
The Clovers 35, 36, 66
The Coasters. 10, 48, 66, 85
The Cooter Ridge
 Armadillo Hunting
 Club.............................. 155
The Coquina Ballroom
 130
The Dark Town Strutters
 Ball 14
The Dells.......................... 78
The Drifters .. 10, 59, 66, 73,
 112, 180
The Ember's Hilton
 Underground 109
The Embers - The Heart
 and Soul of Beach
 Music 4, 119, 167, 218,
 224, 242
The Embers Beach Club
 74
The Embers Beach
 Music Super
 Collaboration............ 201
The Embers Club 151, 229
The Embers Hilton
 Underground ... 107, 109,
 110, 114
The Embers Medley ... 128,
 135
The Embers Roll Eleven
 .... 38, 48

The Embers Sound Emporium.................. 183
The Embers Theme song 54
The Embers: A Landmark Performance 135
The Embers' Christmas Show........................... 212
The Entertainers 153, 165, 173
The Escorts 23
The Fabulous Entertainers... 86, 87, 91
The Fabulous Kays... 152, 176
The Falcons..................... 21
The Fantastic Shakers 197
The Five Jays..... 23, 24, 25
The Five Keys.................. 10
The Five Satins 26
The Four Tops 73, 74
The Impressions ... 48, 224
The Inmates 51
The Intruders................. 78
The Jimmy Castor Bunch 174
The Kays........................ 173
The Landmark Resort Hotel 98, 99, 144, 149, 179
The Legends of Beach 216
The Mad Men 87
The Marcels................... 35
The Monzas 36
The New Embers......... 104

The North Carolina Symphony.................. 179
The North Myrtle Beach Area Historical Museum...................... 153
The Northern Side of Soul............................ 229
The O'Kaysions 73, 108, 202
The Platters 85
The Radiants.................. 66
The Raymen 174
The Rolling Stones 46, 54, 55, 132
The Satellites 22
The Shirelles 59
The Show Must Go On 203, 207, 208
The Showmen 72, 107, 112
The Soul Sensation.... 154
The Spanish Galleon . 133
The Sphinx Club........... 70
The Spinners................. 174
The Supremes 87
The Swinging Embers 33, 36
The Swinging Medallions 203, 207
The Tams . 73, 85, 108, 112, 135
The Temptations...... 53, 66
The Treehouse 95
The Unknown IV........... 51
The Vibrations.......... 54, 55
The Vogues................... 107
The Wax Museum 115, 232

The World's Largest
    Tailgate Party 191
This is Beach Music
    Volume II 198
This One's For You 143,
    146, 165
Tighten Up 74, 76, 81
Tim McCabe 139
TJL Productions 222
Tommy "T-Bird" Smith 73
Try A Little Tenderness
    88
Turley Richards 147
Tweedle Dee 37
U.S. Ambassador' 195
U.S. Olympic Sports
    Festival Opening
    Ceremonies 153
UNC 31
Uncle Sams, ... 89
Underground Atlanta . 86,
    91
Up On The Roof 54, 114
Vacation Live At The
    Landmark 147
Vietnam War 74
Village Theatre 23
Vintage Embers 1958-
    1969 206
Virginia 118
Virginia Beach 124
Virginia Port Festival . 151
Vivaldi Meets The
    Embers 179
W.C. Rogers 155
W.H. King Drug
    Company 40, 41

WABC 44
Wadsworth Wrecking
    Company 83
Wahoo McDaniels 109,
    110
Walk On By 66
Walk to the Marches .. 181
Walking Up a One-Way
    Street 113
Washington, NC 68
Wastin' My Love On You
    208
Watch Out Girl 75, 76, 231
Waylon Jones 252
Wayne Free .. 202, 206, 208,
    218, 225, 242, 252
WCFL 44
We Made Them Dance
    .... 200, 201
Weejuns 51, 68
Weekend 178
Weekend Medley 178
West Palm Beach 189
What Kind of Fool 114
What You Do To Me 52,
    154
What'd I Say 38
Where Did I Go Wrong 66,
    231
White Christmas 211
Why Did You Leave Me
    115
Wigan Casino 228, 231
William Street
    Elementary School 7, 15
William Tell Overture . 182

Williams Lake Dance Club 224
Willie McDougal 252
Willie Nelson 93
Willie Tee 66
Wilmington 162
Wilson landmark 195
Wilson Pickett................ 59
Wilson, NC....................... 36
Wilson, North Carolina. 6
Wine Spo-De-O-Dee 10, 65
Winston-Salem............ 108
Winter Wonderland...... 32
Wish You Didn't Have To Go 160
With Love 198
WKIX...45, 46, 47, 50, 67, 92, 229, 233
WKYC 44

WLAC.................... 10, 32, 44
WNMB 152
Wolfman Jack................ 44
Wolfpack.......................... 53
Wolverhampton's Catacombs Venue .. 231
Woodland Lake................ 9
WQXI 119
WRAL Radio 24
WRAL TV 109
WTVD 33
Wurlitzer electric piano 27
XERF 44
You Are So Beautiful 109, 118
You Can't Sit Down 28
You Got What I Got 66
Zaymin Records .. 147, 179

www.ingramcontent.com/pod-product-compliance
Lightning Source LLC
Chambersburg PA
CBHW030546080526
44585CB00012B/272